Algorithm Optimization: Solve Programming Challenges with Efficiency

A Step-by-Step Guide to Optimizing Algorithms for Performance

MIGUEL FARMER

RAFAEL SANDERS

Table of Content

TABLE OF CONTENTS

INTRODUCTION

In today's fast-paced and increasingly interconnected world, the ability to design efficient algorithms is more important than ever. Whether you're building a mobile app, developing an embedded system, or designing a high-performance cloud service, the performance of your algorithms directly impacts user experience, operational efficiency, and even cost-effectiveness. Algorithm optimization is the key to solving problems faster, using fewer resources, and scaling systems to meet the ever-growing demands of modern applications.

This book, *Algorithm Optimization: Techniques, Trends, and Real-World Applications*, aims to provide a comprehensive guide to understanding and mastering the art of algorithm optimization. It is designed for developers, engineers, data scientists, and anyone looking to improve the efficiency and performance of their algorithms across different domains. Whether you're a beginner seeking to understand the basics or an experienced professional aiming to refine your skills, this book provides the tools and knowledge you need to optimize algorithms for various use cases and industries.

The Importance of Algorithm Optimization

At its core, **algorithm optimization** is about making programs run faster and more efficiently. It's about minimizing the computational resources required—whether time (speed),

6

memory, or energy—while maintaining or even improving the quality of the result. In an age of **big data, real-time processing**, and **distributed systems**, poorly optimized algorithms can quickly become bottlenecks, leading to slow performance, excessive energy consumption, or wasted resources.

Optimizing algorithms involves understanding how they scale and how they behave with large inputs or complex operations. The goal is not always to make the algorithm "the fastest" or "the most memory-efficient" in all cases, but to find the right balance between performance and resources, taking into account real-world constraints.

What to Expect from This Book

This book is divided into several chapters, each focusing on different aspects of algorithm optimization. We start by introducing foundational concepts such as **time complexity**, **space complexity**, and **algorithm design patterns**, before diving into more specialized optimization techniques applicable in various fields, such as **graph algorithms, dynamic programming**, and **machine learning**.

You'll explore the **theory** behind algorithm optimization and learn practical techniques that can be applied in real-world applications. This includes optimization strategies for **distributed systems, cloud computing, mobile apps, IoT devices**, and **embedded** systems—all of which require unique approaches to ensure efficiency in environments with limited resources or demanding real-time constraints.

Key Features of the Book:

Core Optimization Principles: Understanding the basics of algorithm design and optimization, including **Big-O notation, time complexity analysis**, and **space complexity considerations**.

Practical Techniques: Hands-on strategies like **data partitioning, caching, dynamic programming**, and **memoization** to enhance performance.

Real-World Case Studies: In-depth examples from industries such as **finance, healthcare**, and **e-commerce**, showing how optimization techniques are applied in real systems.

Emerging Trends: Exploration of cutting-edge technologies, including **machine learning** and **quantum computing**, and how they're revolutionizing optimization.

Industry-Specific Insights: From **fraud detection** to **recommendation systems**, you'll see how algorithm optimization drives innovation in sectors where speed and accuracy are paramount.

Who This Book Is For

This book is intended for anyone interested in optimizing algorithms for performance and efficiency. Whether you're just starting in the world of programming or you're an experienced developer, this book will provide you with practical insights and knowledge to design better, faster algorithms.

Developers who want to write more efficient code, reduce the overhead of their systems, and scale their applications.

Data Scientists and **Machine Learning Engineers** who need to optimize models and algorithms for real-time prediction or large-scale data processing.

Embedded Systems Engineers working on resource-constrained devices, seeking ways to reduce memory and processing requirements while maintaining high performance.

Students and Learners who are studying algorithm design and optimization techniques and want a deeper understanding of how these concepts apply to real-world problems.

A Comprehensive and Practical Approach

Each chapter of the book is structured to provide you with both **theoretical foundations** and **practical applications**. After explaining the key concepts and techniques, we dive into real-world examples, offering practical solutions to optimization problems faced in industries like **finance, healthcare, e-commerce**, and more. This blend of theory and practice ensures that you not only understand the principles behind algorithm optimization but also know how to apply them in real-world scenarios.

Looking Ahead: The Future of Algorithm Optimization

The field of algorithm optimization is continuously evolving. With the rise of **artificial intelligence, big data, distributed computing**, and **quantum computing**, the future holds many exciting challenges and opportunities. The techniques and tools we use today will evolve, but the core principles of efficient algorithm design will remain foundational. As new technologies like **machine learning, blockchain**, and **quantum computing** emerge, they will shape the next generation of optimization techniques and paradigms. In this book, we will also explore the trends that will shape the future of algorithm optimization and give you a glimpse into what's next.

Conclusion

In this book, you'll gain the knowledge, tools, and insights to approach algorithm optimization systematically. By understanding both the theoretical and practical aspects of optimization, you'll be well-equipped to tackle performance challenges, whether you're building a small mobile app or designing a large-scale distributed system.

Algorithm optimization is an ongoing journey that requires not just technical skills but also creativity and adaptability. With the ever-changing landscape of technology, optimization techniques will continue to evolve, and the ability to stay ahead of these changes will be critical for the success of modern applications.

By the end of this book, you will be equipped to solve complex problems more efficiently, making your algorithms faster, more scalable, and more reliable, ultimately creating better products, services, and systems.

CHAPTER 1

INTRODUCTION TO ALGORITHM OPTIMIZATION

In the world of programming, **optimization** is a critical concept that focuses on improving the efficiency of an algorithm in terms of its performance. Whether you're working on a simple script or a complex system, understanding and applying algorithm optimization techniques can dramatically enhance the responsiveness and scalability of your application. This chapter will introduce you to the fundamentals of algorithm optimization, explain its importance, and highlight key concepts like time complexity, space complexity, and when it makes sense to optimize.

What is Algorithm Optimization?

Algorithm optimization refers to the process of improving an algorithm to make it more efficient in terms of time (speed) and space (memory usage) while achieving the same result. The goal of optimization is to enhance performance without sacrificing the correctness or the clarity of the algorithm.

Optimization can be applied at various levels, including:

Time optimization: Making an algorithm run faster, often by reducing the number of steps it takes to complete a task.

Space optimization: Reducing the amount of memory or storage an algorithm uses to perform its task.

Optimization does not always mean making the algorithm the fastest or the most memory-efficient—it's about finding the right balance based on the application's requirements. Sometimes, a slight sacrifice in one area can lead to significant gains in the other.

Importance of Performance and Efficiency in Programming

The **performance** and **efficiency** of an algorithm play a key role in the overall quality of an application. Here's why optimization matters:

Improved User Experience: For real-time applications (like web apps or games), fast response times are essential for a smooth user experience. A slow algorithm can result in lag, delays, and frustration for users.

Scalability: An optimized algorithm can handle large datasets more effectively. As your application grows and the amount of data increases, a non-optimized algorithm may become unusable due to slow processing times.

Optimizing algorithms ensures your application scales well without running into performance bottlenecks.

Resource Efficiency: With efficient algorithms, your system uses fewer resources (memory, CPU power), which can help reduce costs, especially when running applications on cloud platforms or devices with limited resources (like mobile or embedded systems).

Cost Reduction: Optimizing code reduces resource consumption, lowering hardware and energy costs, especially in environments where computational resources are costly, such as cloud services.

The Trade-offs Between Time Complexity and Space Complexity

When optimizing algorithms, you will often encounter trade-offs between **time complexity** and **space complexity**. These two metrics are essential when evaluating an algorithm's efficiency:

Time Complexity: Refers to how the execution time of an algorithm grows as the input size increases. This is typically measured using Big-O notation (e.g., $O(n)$, $O(\log n)$, $O(n^2)$).

Example: A sorting algorithm with $O(n^2)$ time complexity (like bubble sort) will take much

14

longer to execute for large datasets than one with O(n log n) time complexity (like merge sort).

Space Complexity: Refers to how much memory an algorithm uses relative to the input size. Space complexity also grows with larger inputs, and it is usually measured in terms of the additional memory used (e.g., $O(1)$, $O(n)$, $O(n^2)$).

> **Example**: If an algorithm requires storing a large amount of intermediate data in memory, its space complexity may be higher compared to one that computes results directly.

The Trade-Offs

When optimizing an algorithm, **time** and **space** are often in conflict. Optimizing for one may lead to an increase in the other. Here are some scenarios where these trade-offs occur:

Reducing Time Complexity by Using More Space:

> Example: In dynamic programming, we often store intermediate results in a table (tabulation or memoization) to avoid redundant calculations. This results in a space complexity increase, but it drastically reduces the time complexity.

Space-time trade-off: Sometimes, an algorithm that caches intermediate results can speed up future calculations at the cost of using more memory.

Reducing Space Complexity by Using More Time:

Example: Algorithms that don't store intermediate results in memory and re-compute them as needed (e.g., recursive algorithms) tend to use less memory but take more time due to repeated computations.

Time-space trade-off: Recursion is a typical example where you may save space by not storing extra data, but the time complexity could increase because of repeated function calls.

The key is to balance these two factors based on the problem you're trying to solve and the constraints of your environment. Sometimes it's acceptable to use a bit more space for a faster algorithm, while in other situations, minimizing memory usage might be critical.

Understanding the Context: When to Optimize and When Not To

Not every problem requires optimization. In some cases, attempting to optimize an algorithm prematurely can lead to over-engineering or unnecessary complexity. Here are some guidelines on when to optimize and when not to:

When to Optimize:

Scalability is Critical: When you know the input size will be large or will increase over time (e.g., large-scale web applications or data-processing systems).

Real-Time Requirements: For systems that require immediate feedback or updates, such as gaming or real-time data streaming.

High Resource Consumption: If your application is consuming excessive memory or CPU power, optimization may be necessary to keep operational costs low.

Performance Bottlenecks: If you identify specific parts of your program that are slowing down the entire system, those are the areas that should be optimized.

When Not to Optimize:

Premature Optimization: Don't optimize until you understand where the bottlenecks are. Premature optimization can make the code more complex and harder to maintain without yielding significant performance benefits.

Simple Problems: For smaller applications or problems with limited input sizes, the overhead of optimization may outweigh its benefits.

Code Clarity: It's important to balance optimization with maintainability. Sometimes, writing clear and understandable code is more important than optimizing for performance, especially when the performance gains are marginal.

Remember the Principle of Optimization: **"Make it work, make it right, then make it fast."** First, ensure the algorithm works correctly, then improve the clarity and structure of the code, and only then focus on performance optimization if necessary.

Basic Terminology in Algorithm Optimization

Before diving into specific techniques for optimizing algorithms, it's important to understand some key terminology:

Big-O Notation: A mathematical notation used to describe the upper bound of an algorithm's time or space complexity. It gives an approximation of the performance relative to the input size.

18

Example: O(n) means that as the input grows, the time or space required grows linearly.

Worst-case, Best-case, and Average-case:

Worst-case: The maximum time or space an algorithm requires for any input size.

Best-case: The minimum time or space an algorithm requires for any input size.

Average-case: The expected time or space an algorithm will require, averaged over all possible inputs.

Amortized Analysis: A technique used to analyze the average time complexity of operations over a sequence of operations, especially when some operations may take longer than others. It's often used for data structures like stacks or queues.

Space-Time Trade-off: Refers to the decision-making process when choosing between an algorithm that uses more space or one that uses more time. It's a balancing act depending on what your system prioritizes.

Conclusion

In this chapter, we introduced the core concepts of **algorithm optimization**, emphasizing the importance of performance and efficiency in programming. Understanding the balance between **time complexity** and **space complexity** is key to writing optimal algorithms, but knowing when to optimize—and when not to—is just as critical. By focusing on **real-world use cases**, we can better understand how these optimization techniques are applied in practical scenarios.

As we move forward in this book, we will explore various strategies for improving the efficiency of algorithms, using practical examples and exercises to ensure that you understand how to implement these techniques effectively.

CHAPTER 2

TIME COMPLEXITY AND SPACE COMPLEXITY BASICS

In this chapter, we will explore two fundamental concepts that form the foundation of algorithm optimization: **time complexity** and **space complexity**. These concepts help us evaluate how efficient an algorithm is in terms of the time it takes to run and the amount of memory it uses, which is crucial for making informed decisions when optimizing algorithms.

Big-O Notation Explained

Big-O notation is a mathematical concept used to describe the upper bound of an algorithm's complexity in terms of time (time complexity) or space (space complexity). It provides an abstraction that helps us understand how an algorithm's performance grows relative to the input size, and it allows us to compare the efficiency of different algorithms.

Big-O notation expresses the worst-case scenario of an algorithm's growth rate, ignoring constant factors and lower-order terms. It helps us focus on the primary factor that affects the performance of the algorithm as the size of the input increases.

Here are some common Big-O notations and what they represent:

O(1): Constant time complexity. The algorithm's runtime or space usage does not depend on the input size. No matter how large the input, the algorithm will perform the same number of operations.

> **Example**: Accessing an element in a list by index.

O(log n): Logarithmic time complexity. The algorithm's runtime grows logarithmically as the input size increases. This is typical of algorithms that divide the problem in half with each step, such as binary search.

> **Example**: Binary search in a sorted array.

O(n): Linear time complexity. The algorithm's runtime increases linearly with the input size.

> **Example**: A loop that iterates through each element in an array.

O(n log n): Linearithmic time complexity. This is common for more efficient sorting algorithms like merge sort and quicksort.

> **Example**: Merge sort, quicksort.

O(n^2): Quadratic time complexity. The algorithm's runtime grows quadratically as the input size increases, which is often seen in algorithms with nested loops.

Example: Bubble sort, insertion sort.

O(2^n): Exponential time complexity. The algorithm's runtime doubles with each additional element in the input. This is typically seen in algorithms that explore all possible combinations, such as brute-force solutions for combinatorial problems.

Example: Solving the traveling salesman problem via brute force.

O(n!): Factorial time complexity. The algorithm's runtime grows extremely fast as the input size increases. This is seen in problems that require evaluating all permutations of a set.

Example: Solving the traveling salesman problem by evaluating all possible paths.

Big-O notation helps us understand the efficiency of an algorithm, especially for large input sizes. It allows us to compare algorithms and determine which one is more suitable for the task at hand, based on time and memory constraints.

23

Understanding Worst-Case, Best-Case, and Average-Case Complexities

When analyzing the performance of an algorithm, it's essential to understand different scenarios in which it might operate. This can be summarized in three cases:

Worst-Case Complexity:

> This is the maximum time or space the algorithm will take on any input of size n. It is the most commonly used measure for performance, as it gives us an upper bound for the algorithm's behavior.

> **Example**: In a bubble sort, the worst-case scenario occurs when the input list is sorted in reverse order, requiring the maximum number of swaps.

Best-Case Complexity:

> This represents the minimum time or space the algorithm takes, typically when the input is already optimized or in a specific configuration that requires the least processing.

Example: In a bubble sort, the best-case scenario occurs when the input list is already sorted, requiring only a single pass to confirm the order.

Average-Case Complexity:

This represents the expected time or space the algorithm will take on an average input. It is harder to calculate because it requires considering all possible inputs, but it provides a more realistic estimate of an algorithm's performance in typical use.

Example: In quicksort, the average-case complexity assumes that the pivot divides the array fairly evenly.

In many cases, the worst-case complexity is the most important measure to consider, especially when dealing with large datasets, as it guarantees the algorithm will not perform worse than the given bound.

Space Complexity: Memory Usage vs Performance

While time complexity focuses on how long an algorithm takes to run, **space complexity** measures how much memory an algorithm requires relative to the input size. Space complexity is an important factor to consider, especially in environments with

25

limited memory, such as embedded systems, mobile devices, or when handling very large datasets.

Space complexity can be broken down into two types:

Auxiliary Space: The extra space used by the algorithm, excluding the space needed for the input data.

Total Space: The total space used by the algorithm, including the space for the input data and auxiliary space.

Example of Space Complexity Considerations:

O(1): Constant space. An algorithm that uses a fixed amount of memory regardless of the input size.

Example: A function that swaps two numbers.

O(n): Linear space. The algorithm uses space proportional to the input size.

Example: Storing a list of n elements.

O(n^2): Quadratic space. The algorithm uses space proportional to the square of the input size.

Example: Creating a 2D matrix with n rows and n columns.

In practice, reducing space complexity is often as important as reducing time complexity, especially when working with large amounts of data or in environments where memory is constrained.

Real-World Examples to Visualize Time and Space Complexities

Let's visualize time and space complexities with real-world examples.

Time Complexity Example: Searching a Name in a List

Linear Search (O(n)): If you have a list of 1,000 names, and you're searching for a specific name by checking each one in order, the time complexity is O(n), where n is the number of names. If the list grows to 10,000 names, the time taken will increase linearly.

Binary Search (O(log n)): If the list is sorted and you use binary search, the time complexity becomes O(log n), meaning that even if the list grows to millions of items, the number of operations needed grows very slowly (logarithmic growth).

Space Complexity Example: Storing Data

Array (O(n)): If you need to store 1,000 elements, the space complexity is O(n), where n is 1,000.

The amount of memory used will increase linearly as the number of elements increases.

Linked List (O(n)): A linked list also uses $O(n)$ space because you need to store n nodes. However, linked lists may have additional overhead due to pointers between nodes.

Calculating the Complexity of Basic Algorithms

Let's go through the time and space complexities of some basic algorithms.

Bubble Sort ($O(n^2)$ Time, $O(1)$ Space):

Bubble sort repeatedly swaps adjacent elements if they are in the wrong order. For each element, the algorithm makes a number of comparisons proportional to the size of the list, resulting in $O(n^2)$ time complexity. It only requires a small constant amount of extra space, so the space complexity is $O(1)$.

Merge Sort ($O(n \log n)$ Time, $O(n)$ Space):

Merge sort divides the list into two halves and recursively sorts them before merging them back together. The time complexity is $O(n \log n)$

28

because the list is divided in half `log` n times, and each division requires O(n) work to merge the sublists. It uses extra space for the temporary arrays during the merge process, so the space complexity is O(n).

Binary Search (O(log n) Time, O(1) Space):

Binary search repeatedly divides a sorted list in half, looking for a target element. With each division, it reduces the search space by half, resulting in O(log n) time complexity. Since no additional space is used other than the search space, the space complexity is O(1).

Insertion Sort (O(n^2) Time, O(1) Space):

Insertion sort builds the final sorted array one item at a time. It compares each new item with those already sorted and inserts it into the correct position. Its time complexity is O(n^2) due to the nested loops for comparison and insertion, while the space complexity is O(1), as it sorts in place.

Conclusion

In this chapter, we introduced **time complexity** and **space complexity**, two critical concepts for understanding the efficiency of algorithms. We explained how Big-O notation helps us describe the growth rate of algorithms and provided insights into the worst-case, best-case, and average-case complexities. Additionally, we discussed how space complexity can affect an algorithm's performance, particularly in memory-constrained environments.

We also provided real-world examples of how time and space complexities work in practice and demonstrated how to calculate the complexities of basic algorithms. Understanding these concepts will form the foundation for the more advanced optimization techniques that follow in the rest of this book.

A network error occurred. Please check your connection and try again. If this issue persists please contact us through our help center at help.openai.com.

CHAPTER 3

ANALYZING ALGORITHM PERFORMANCE

In this chapter, we will dive into how to **analyze algorithm performance** through profiling and benchmarking. This process is crucial to identify inefficiencies, pinpoint bottlenecks, and ultimately enhance the performance of your algorithms. We'll explore **built-in tools and libraries** available for performance analysis, how to **identify performance bottlenecks** in your code, and how to **measure the performance** of an algorithm effectively.

Profiling and Benchmarking Algorithms

Before we can optimize any algorithm, we need to understand where it can be improved. This is where **profiling** and **benchmarking** come into play.

> **Profiling** refers to the process of measuring the runtime of different parts of your program. Profiling helps you identify which functions or parts of your algorithm are taking the most time or consuming the most resources.

Benchmarking is the practice of testing the performance of an algorithm under different conditions, typically by running it with varying input sizes or across different systems. It provides concrete measurements of how well an algorithm performs.

Profiling Algorithms

Profiling allows us to track and evaluate the performance of an algorithm and determine which areas need optimization. Profiling tools give detailed insights into where your code spends most of its time, and they can also identify memory usage issues.

1. Using Python's Built-in cProfile

Python provides a built-in tool called **cProfile** for profiling Python code. It can be used to gather data on the function calls made during the execution of a program.

Example: Profiling a Simple Algorithm

Consider the following function to calculate the sum of a list:

```python
import time

def sum_list(lst):
    result = 0
```

```
    for num in lst:
        result += num
    return result


# Benchmarking with time
start_time = time.time()
sum_list(range(100000))
print("Time taken:", time.time() - start_time)
```

To profile this code with `cProfile`, use the following:

```
python
```

```
import cProfile

def sum_list(lst):
    result = 0
    for num in lst:
        result += num
    return result


cProfile.run('sum_list(range(100000))')
```

This will give output like:

```
pgsql
```

```
        100001 function calls in 0.023 seconds

    Ordered by: standard name
```

33

```
   ncalls    tottime    percall    cumtime    percall
filename:lineno(function)
        1     0.000      0.000      0.023      0.023
<ipython-input-1-7588f5c20f38>:1(sum_list)
        1     0.000      0.000      0.023      0.023
{built-in method builtins.exec}
        1     0.000      0.000      0.023      0.023
<string>:1(<module>)
   100000     0.023      0.000      0.023      0.000
<ipython-input-1-7588f5c20f38>:3(<listcomp>)
```

This output gives us a breakdown of how much time was spent in the function calls, including:

ncalls: Number of calls to the function

tottime: Total time spent in the function (excluding time spent in sub-functions)

cumtime: Cumulative time spent in the function and all sub-functions

By analyzing this, we can see that the function spends a significant amount of time inside the loop and performing the sum operation. Profiling helps pinpoint areas where time is spent and highlights opportunities for optimization.

2. Visualizing Performance with `SnakeViz`

SnakeViz is a visualization tool for profiling results in Python. It takes `cProfile` output and visualizes it in an interactive, graphical format.

To install and use SnakeViz:

bash

```
pip install snakeviz
```

Then, profile your program and visualize the results:

bash

```
python -m cProfile -o output.prof my_program.py
snakeviz output.prof
```

This will generate an interactive visualization, helping you better understand which parts of your program consume the most resources.

Benchmarking Algorithms

Benchmarking helps you understand how your algorithm performs under different conditions, including varying input sizes or system configurations. The goal is to compare the performance of different algorithms and configurations to find the most efficient solution.

1. Using Python's time Module for Simple Benchmarking

For simple benchmarking, Python's **time** module is a quick and easy way to measure how long an algorithm takes to execute.

Example:

```python
import time

start = time.time()

# Your algorithm code here, e.g., a sorting function
sorted_list     =     sorted(range(1000000),
reverse=True)

end = time.time()

print(f"Execution time: {end - start} seconds")
```

This will give the time taken by the algorithm to run, but it only provides basic information. It's useful for quick benchmarks but lacks advanced features like measuring CPU time or function call statistics.

36

2. Using `timeit` for More Precise Benchmarking

The **timeit** module provides a more accurate way to benchmark small code snippets by running them multiple times to account for variations in execution time.

Example:

python

```
import timeit

# Time a function
execution_time                          =
timeit.timeit('sorted(range(1000000),
reverse=True)', number=100)
print(f"Average execution time: {execution_time}
seconds")
```

Here, the function is executed 100 times, and the average time taken for each execution is measured. This gives a more stable and precise benchmark, especially for small code snippets.

Identifying Bottlenecks in Your Code

A **bottleneck** in an algorithm refers to a part of the program that limits the overall performance, usually because it's slow or inefficient. Identifying bottlenecks is a crucial step in optimization.

1. Profiling and Analyzing

Use the profiling tools we discussed earlier (`cProfile`, `SnakeViz`, `timeit`) to identify where your program spends most of its time. If a particular function or method takes up a large portion of the execution time, it may be a bottleneck that requires optimization.

2. Common Bottlenecks to Look For

Inefficient Loops: Nested loops or unnecessary repeated calculations can significantly increase time complexity.

Excessive Memory Allocation: Large data structures or frequent memory allocations can cause high space complexity and slow down the algorithm.

Inefficient Data Structures: Using the wrong data structures for your task can lead to unnecessary overhead. For example, using a list for frequent lookups when a dictionary would be more efficient.

3. Example: Identifying a Bottleneck in Sorting

Let's consider two sorting algorithms: **bubble sort** and **merge sort**. Bubble sort has O(n^2) time complexity, while merge sort has O(n log n). Let's compare their performance:

```python
import timeit

bubble_sort_time                               =
timeit.timeit('bubble_sort(list(range(1000)))',
setup="from    __main__   import   bubble_sort",
number=10)
merge_sort_time                                =
timeit.timeit('sorted(list(range(1000)))',
number=10)


print(f"Bubble   Sort   Time:   {bubble_sort_time}
seconds")
print(f"Merge   Sort   Time:   {merge_sort_time}
seconds")
```

By benchmarking both algorithms, we can clearly identify that bubble sort is much slower than merge sort for larger inputs, making it the bottleneck in performance.

How to Measure the Performance of an Algorithm

To measure the performance of an algorithm, we need to consider both time and space. Here's how you can go about it:

1. Time Complexity Measurement

Execution Time: Measure how long an algorithm takes to complete using `time`, `timeit`, or profiling tools.

Big-O Notation: Use theoretical analysis of your algorithm to estimate its time complexity. For example, a sorting algorithm like quicksort has an average-case time complexity of O(n log n).

2. Space Complexity Measurement

Memory Usage: Measure how much memory an algorithm consumes using tools like Python's `sys.getsizeof()` or memory profilers like **memory_profiler**.

Example:

```python
import sys

lst = [i for i in range(100000)]
print(sys.getsizeof(lst))
```

This will tell you how much memory is used by the list in bytes. For larger objects or custom data structures, this can help you understand how much memory your algorithm is consuming.

3. Profiling Space Complexity

To profile space complexity, use tools like **memory_profiler** to get an idea of how memory usage grows as your algorithm executes.

```bash
bash
```

```
pip install memory_profiler
python
```

```python
from memory_profiler import profile

@profile
def my_algorithm():
    lst = [i for i in range(100000)]
    return lst

my_algorithm()
```

This will provide detailed information on the memory used during the execution of your function, helping you identify potential areas for optimization.

Conclusion

In this chapter, we explored the process of **profiling and benchmarking algorithms** to evaluate their performance. We discussed tools like **cProfile**, **timeit**, and **SnakeViz** to measure time complexity and identify bottlenecks in your code. Additionally, we explored techniques for measuring space complexity, understanding common bottlenecks, and how to analyze and optimize the performance of your algorithms. By effectively using these tools and strategies, you can ensure that your algorithms are efficient and ready for real-world challenges.

CHAPTER 4

SORTING ALGORITHMS AND THEIR OPTIMIZATIONS

Sorting is one of the most fundamental operations in computer science, and it serves as the foundation for many algorithms and applications. Whether you're working with databases, search engines, or simple data structures, knowing how to choose and optimize the right sorting algorithm for your use case is essential for efficiency.

In this chapter, we'll cover the following topics:

An overview of common sorting algorithms (Bubble Sort, Quick Sort, Merge Sort, etc.)

How to optimize these sorting algorithms for different use cases

A comparison of time complexities for sorting algorithms

Real-world examples: when and why to choose a specific sorting algorithm

Overview of Common Sorting Algorithms

Sorting algorithms are designed to arrange data in a specific order (usually ascending or descending). Here, we'll discuss some of the most common sorting algorithms, their approaches, and when they are typically used.

1. Bubble Sort

Bubble Sort is a simple comparison-based algorithm where each pair of adjacent elements is compared and swapped if they are in the wrong order. This process is repeated for all elements in the list until the list is sorted.

Time Complexity:

Best Case: $O(n)$ (when the list is already sorted)

Worst Case: $O(n^2)$ (when the list is in reverse order)

Average Case: $O(n^2)$

Space Complexity: $O(1)$ (in-place sorting)

Pros: Easy to understand and implement; works well for small lists.

Cons: Inefficient for large datasets due to its quadratic time complexity.

Example: Sorting a small list of numbers with Bubble Sort:

python

```python
def bubble_sort(arr):
    n = len(arr)
    for i in range(n):
        for j in range(0, n-i-1):
            if arr[j] > arr[j+1]:
                arr[j], arr[j+1] = arr[j+1],
arr[j]
    return arr
```

2. Quick Sort

Quick Sort is a divide-and-conquer algorithm that selects a "pivot" element from the array and partitions the other elements into two sub-arrays: elements less than the pivot and elements greater than the pivot. The sub-arrays are then recursively sorted.

Time Complexity:

Best and Average Case: O(n log n)

Worst Case: O(n^2) (when the pivot is consistently the smallest or largest element)

Space Complexity: O(log n) (due to recursion stack)

45

Pros: Very efficient in practice for large datasets; in-place sorting (uses less memory).

Cons: Worst-case time complexity can be $O(n^2)$, but this is rare if the pivot is chosen well.

Example: Quick Sort in Python:

python

```
def quick_sort(arr):
    if len(arr) <= 1:
        return arr
    pivot = arr[len(arr) // 2]
    left = [x for x in arr if x < pivot]
    middle = [x for x in arr if x == pivot]
    right = [x for x in arr if x > pivot]
    return    quick_sort(left)    +    middle    +
quick_sort(right)
```

3. Merge Sort

Merge Sort is another divide-and-conquer algorithm that splits the array into two halves, recursively sorts them, and then merges them back together. It ensures that the array is always divided into sub-arrays, and then each sub-array is merged in sorted order.

Time Complexity:

Best, Worst, and Average Case: O(n log n)

Space Complexity: O(n) (due to the space used by the temporary arrays)

Pros: Always performs in O(n log n) time; stable sort (preserves the order of equal elements).

Cons: Uses additional memory for temporary arrays.

Example: Merge Sort in Python:

python

```python
def merge_sort(arr):
    if len(arr) > 1:
        mid = len(arr) // 2
        left_half = arr[:mid]
        right_half = arr[mid:]

        merge_sort(left_half)
        merge_sort(right_half)

        i = j = k = 0
        while i < len(left_half) and j <
len(right_half):
            if left_half[i] < right_half[j]:
                arr[k] = left_half[i]
                i += 1
            else:
```

```
            arr[k] = right_half[j]
            j += 1
        k += 1

    while i < len(left_half):
        arr[k] = left_half[i]
        i += 1
        k += 1

    while j < len(right_half):
        arr[k] = right_half[j]
        j += 1
        k += 1
    return arr
```

4. Insertion Sort

Insertion Sort builds the sorted array one element at a time by picking the next element and inserting it into the correct position relative to the already-sorted part of the array.

Time Complexity:

Best Case: O(n) (when the list is already sorted)

Worst Case: O(n²) (when the list is in reverse order)

Average Case: O(n²)

Space Complexity: O(1) (in-place sorting)

Pros: Simple and efficient for small datasets or nearly sorted data.

Cons: Inefficient for larger datasets.

Example: Insertion Sort in Python:

python

```
def insertion_sort(arr):
    for i in range(1, len(arr)):
        key = arr[i]
        j = i - 1
        while j >= 0 and key < arr[j]:
            arr[j + 1] = arr[j]
            j -= 1
        arr[j + 1] = key
    return arr
```

Optimizing Sorting Algorithms for Different Use Cases

Choosing the right sorting algorithm often depends on the specific problem you're dealing with. Here are some general rules to help you choose the best sorting algorithm based on your use case:

Use Quick Sort:

When you need a fast, general-purpose sorting algorithm for large datasets.

Quick Sort is typically faster than Merge Sort and Insertion Sort due to its smaller constant factors.

It's not ideal when the input array is nearly sorted or contains many duplicate values.

Use Merge Sort:

When you need stable sorting (preserving the order of equal elements).

When your data is too large to fit into memory, as Merge Sort can be implemented in an external sorting fashion.

When you need guaranteed O(n log n) performance.

Use Bubble Sort or Insertion Sort:

For small or nearly sorted datasets, where the simplicity of the algorithm outweighs its inefficiency in larger datasets.

Insertion Sort is particularly useful when the array is nearly sorted because it can perform better than other algorithms like Bubble Sort for such cases.

Use Heap Sort:

When you need an in-place, non-recursive sorting algorithm with O(n log n) time complexity.

Heap Sort guarantees worst-case performance and is often used in systems where consistent time performance is critical.

Time Complexity Comparisons of Sorting Algorithms

Here is a comparison of the time complexities of the sorting algorithms discussed:

Sorting Algorithm	Best Case Time Complexity	Average Case Time Complexity	Worst Case Time Complexity	Space Complexity
Bubble Sort	O(n)	O(n²)	O(n²)	O(1)
Quick Sort	O(n log n)	O(n log n)	O(n²)	O(log n)
Merge Sort	O(n log n)	O(n log n)	O(n log n)	O(n)
Insertion Sort	O(n)	O(n²)	O(n²)	O(1)

51

Sorting Algorithm	Best Case Time Complexity	Average Case Time Complexity	Worst Case Time Complexity	Space Complexity
Heap Sort	O(n log n)	O(n log n)	O(n log n)	O(1)

Real-World Examples: When and Why to Choose a Specific Sorting Algorithm

Sorting for Large Datasets in Memory:

Quick Sort is often the go-to choice for general-purpose sorting because of its average-case O(n log n) time complexity and in-place sorting (low memory overhead). However, its worst-case complexity (O(n²)) means that it can degrade if the pivot is poorly chosen.

Merge Sort is used when consistent performance is needed, as it guarantees O(n log n) in all cases. It's also preferred in cases where stable sorting is required (e.g., sorting by name after sorting by age).

Sorting for Small Datasets:

Insertion Sort can be a good choice for small datasets or arrays that are nearly sorted because of its lower overhead compared to more complex algorithms. It works well when the number of elements is small, say in the range of 10-100.

Sorting for Real-Time Systems:

Heap Sort is suitable for real-time systems where you cannot afford to have an algorithm that can take quadratic time in the worst case. It guarantees O(n log n) time complexity and doesn't require additional memory for recursion, making it ideal for systems where consistent and predictable performance is needed.

Sorting Large Datasets Externally:

Merge Sort is often the algorithm of choice when dealing with external sorting, where the dataset is too large to fit into memory. Merge Sort's ability to merge sorted sublists makes it a great fit for situations where data is read from disk in chunks and then merged together.

Conclusion

Sorting is a fundamental algorithmic task, and understanding the strengths and weaknesses of different sorting algorithms is essential for optimizing your program. In this chapter, we've covered a variety of sorting algorithms—**Bubble Sort**, **Quick Sort**, **Merge Sort**, **Insertion Sort**, and **Heap Sort**—and explored when and why to choose each one based on your specific needs. By understanding the time complexities and space requirements of these algorithms, as well as the trade-offs between them, you can make more informed decisions about which sorting algorithm to implement in different scenarios.

CHAPTER 5

SEARCHING ALGORITHMS AND THEIR OPTIMIZATIONS

Searching is another fundamental operation in computer science, and optimizing searching algorithms is critical for efficient data retrieval. Whether you're working with small or large datasets, choosing the right algorithm and optimization technique can have a huge impact on performance. In this chapter, we will cover the following topics:

Linear Search vs Binary Search

Optimizing Searching in Large Datasets

Introduction to Hashing Techniques and Their Benefits

Example: Optimizing Search in Databases

Linear Search vs Binary Search

Two of the most common searching algorithms are **linear search** and **binary search**. Each algorithm has its own advantages and limitations, depending on the context in which it's used.

1. Linear Search

Linear search is the simplest searching algorithm. It works by checking each element in a list one by one until it finds the target element or reaches the end of the list. If the element is found, the algorithm returns its index; otherwise, it returns a failure indication (e.g., None or -1).

Time Complexity: O(n), where n is the number of elements in the list.

Space Complexity: O(1) (in-place search).

When to Use Linear Search:

When the list is **unsorted**, or if the list is small.

For small datasets or when searching through lists that are frequently modified.

Example: Implementing linear search in Python:

python

```python
def linear_search(arr, target):
    for i, value in enumerate(arr):
        if value == target:
            return i  # Return the index if found
    return -1   # Return -1 if target is not in
the list
```

```
arr = [5, 3, 8, 4, 2]
target = 4
result = linear_search(arr, target)
print(f"Target found at index: {result}")
```

2. Binary Search

Binary search is a more efficient algorithm for **sorted arrays**. It works by repeatedly dividing the search interval in half. If the target value is smaller than the middle element, the search continues on the left half; otherwise, it continues on the right half. This process repeats until the target element is found or the interval is empty.

Time Complexity: O(log n), where n is the number of elements in the list.

Space Complexity: O(1) for iterative implementation, O(log n) for recursive implementation (due to recursion stack).

When to Use Binary Search:

When the list is **sorted**, and you need to search quickly in a large dataset.

In cases where performance is critical and data is static or doesn't change frequently.

Example: Implementing binary search in Python:

```python
python

def binary_search(arr, target):
    low, high = 0, len(arr) - 1
    while low <= high:
        mid = (low + high) // 2
        if arr[mid] == target:
            return mid   # Return index of the target if found
        elif arr[mid] < target:
            low = mid + 1
        else:
            high = mid - 1
    return -1   # Return -1 if target is not in the list

arr = [1, 3, 4, 6, 8, 10]
target = 6
result = binary_search(arr, target)
print(f"Target found at index: {result}")
```

Key Differences Between Linear Search and Binary Search:

Time Complexity: Linear search has O(n) complexity, meaning it checks every element. Binary search, on the other hand, has O(log n) complexity, making it much faster for large datasets (but only when the data is sorted).

Pre-requisite: Binary search requires the data to be sorted, while linear search can be used with unsorted data.

Optimizing Searching in Large Datasets

When working with large datasets, both **time complexity** and **space complexity** become crucial factors to consider. Here are several optimization techniques that can improve search operations in large datasets:

1. **Using** **Indexing**:
For large datasets, **indexing** can greatly speed up search operations. Indexes create additional data structures that allow for faster lookups.

> In a **database**, indexes are used to quickly locate rows based on certain column values.

> In an **array**, you can use techniques like **binary search trees** or **hash tables** for faster searching.

Example: In a database, an index on a column allows the database management system (DBMS) to quickly find rows with specific values, rather than scanning the entire table.

2. **Binary** **Search** **on** **Sorted** **Data**:
For static or read-heavy data, sorting the data once and then using

binary search can be highly effective. Although sorting has O(n log n) time complexity, it makes subsequent searches much faster.

3.   Divide   and   Conquer: In cases of large datasets, using a divide-and-conquer strategy can be beneficial. Techniques like **merge sort** and **quick sort** are optimized algorithms that can help split the data into smaller subsets, making searching more efficient in those smaller sections.

4.   Hashing: Hashing is a technique that maps data to a fixed-size value, typically using a hash function. It allows for **constant-time complexity (O(1))** for lookups, making it incredibly efficient for large datasets.

Introduction to Hashing Techniques and Their Benefits

Hashing is a technique used to map data to a fixed-size value, typically a **hash code**, that can be used for quick lookup, insertion, and deletion operations. It uses a **hash function** to compute an index into an array (called a hash table or hash map) where the desired value is stored.

Benefits of Hashing:

O(1) Time Complexity: Hashing allows for **constant time** lookups and insertions on average, which is much faster than O(n) or O(log n) time complexities.

Efficient Data Retrieval: Hashing helps reduce the time needed to search for specific elements, especially in large datasets or large key-value stores.

Collisions: A collision occurs when two distinct keys produce the same hash code. Good hash functions minimize collisions, and collision resolution techniques like **chaining** or **open addressing** help handle these cases.

Hash Table Example

A hash table (or hash map) stores key-value pairs and uses a hash function to map keys to indices in an array. If two keys map to the same index (a collision), the hash table will handle it using a technique like chaining or open addressing.

Example of a hash table in Python:

python

```
class HashTable:
    def __init__(self):
        self.table = [None] * 10  # Create a table
with 10 slots

    def hash_function(self, key):
        return hash(key) % len(self.table)    #
Simple hash function using modulus
```

```
    def insert(self, key, value):
        index = self.hash_function(key)
        if self.table[index] is None:
            self.table[index] = (key, value)
        else:
            # Handle collision (simple example)
            print(f"Collision occurred at index
{index}, handling manually")
            self.table[index] = (key, value)

    def search(self, key):
        index = self.hash_function(key)
        if          self.table[index]           and
self.table[index][0] == key:
            return    self.table[index][1]       #
Return the value
        return None   # Key not found


# Example usage:
ht = HashTable()
ht.insert("apple", 10)
ht.insert("banana", 20)
print(ht.search("apple"))   # Output: 10
print(ht.search("banana"))  # Output: 20
```

In the example above, the hash_function maps each key to an index in the hash table, allowing for **constant-time** insertion and search.

Example: Optimizing Search in Databases

In large databases, efficient search operations are crucial for performance. **Indexes** are often used to optimize search queries.

B-tree Index: A self-balancing tree data structure that keeps data sorted and allows for binary search-like operations. It's widely used for database indexing.

Hash Index: A type of index that uses a hash table to store keys and their corresponding data. This provides extremely fast lookups but is not suitable for range queries.

Database Example: Searching in a SQL Database

Consider a scenario where we need to search for a user in a database by their username. Without an index, a database query would require scanning each row in the table, resulting in **O(n)** time complexity. By adding an index to the `username` column, we reduce the time complexity to **O(log n)**, making the search operation significantly faster.

```sql

-- Creating an index on the username column
CREATE INDEX idx_username ON users(username);
```

```
-- Now searching for a user by username becomes
faster
SELECT * FROM users WHERE username = 'johndoe';
```

By creating an index on the `username` column, the database management system can use a more efficient search strategy (e.g., a B-tree), drastically reducing the time required for this search.

Conclusion

In this chapter, we've explored key searching algorithms such as **linear search** and **binary search**, compared their time complexities, and discussed when to use each. We also looked at **optimizing search in large datasets**, including the importance of **hashing** and how **hash tables** can be used to achieve constant-time search operations. Additionally, we examined real-world applications of search optimizations in contexts like **databases**, where indexing plays a vital role in improving performance.

Choosing the right search algorithm or data structure for your use case is critical for ensuring that your application remains efficient and scalable. As datasets grow larger, optimization techniques like hashing and indexing become increasingly important for maintaining fast search times.

CHAPTER 6

RECURSION VS ITERATION: OPTIMIZING RECURSIVE ALGORITHMS

Recursion and iteration are two fundamental approaches to problem-solving in computer science. Both are useful for different scenarios, but when it comes to performance optimization, recursion can sometimes lead to inefficiencies. In this chapter, we will explore the concept of **recursion** and **iteration**, explain when to use each, and discuss how to optimize recursive algorithms for performance. We will also dive into two important optimization techniques: **tail recursion optimization** and **memoization**. To illustrate these concepts, we'll walk through a real-world example of optimizing the Fibonacci sequence generation.

The Concept of Recursion and When to Use It

Recursion is a technique where a function calls itself in order to solve a problem. The idea is to break down a problem into smaller, more manageable sub-problems, and solve those recursively until the base case is reached.

Basic Structure of a Recursive Function

A typical recursive function consists of:

Base Case: The stopping condition that prevents infinite recursion.

Recursive Case: The part of the function that calls itself with a simpler version of the original problem.

Example: Factorial Function (Recursive Approach)

The factorial of a number n, denoted as n!, is the product of all integers from 1 to n. It can be defined recursively:

Base Case: n! = 1 when n = 0

Recursive Case: n! = n * (n-1)!

python

```python
def factorial(n):
    if n == 0:
        return 1
    else:
        return n * factorial(n - 1)
```

In the above example, the function keeps calling itself with decreasing values of n until it reaches the base case of n = 0.

When to Use Recursion

Divide-and-conquer problems: Problems like quicksort, merge sort, and binary search are naturally suited for recursion.

Tree and graph traversal: Recursive algorithms are ideal for problems involving hierarchical structures like trees (e.g., tree traversal) and graphs (e.g., depth-first search).

Mathematical problems: Many mathematical functions, like factorial, Fibonacci numbers, and combinations, have natural recursive definitions.

However, while recursion is a powerful tool, it comes with some drawbacks, such as **stack overflow** (due to deep recursion) and **inefficiency** (due to redundant calculations or excessive function calls).

How to Optimize Recursive Algorithms for Performance

Recursive algorithms can sometimes lead to performance issues, especially if the recursion depth becomes too large or if the algorithm performs redundant calculations. Here are some ways to optimize recursive algorithms:

1. Reduce Redundant Calculations

One common problem with naive recursion is that the same sub-problems are solved multiple times. This happens frequently in problems like the **Fibonacci sequence** or the **n-th triangular number**, where recursive calls repeatedly solve the same problem with the same inputs.

2. Tail Recursion Optimization

Tail recursion is a special type of recursion where the recursive call is the last operation in the function. Tail recursion is particularly useful because some programming languages or compilers can optimize tail-recursive functions by reusing the current function's stack frame instead of creating a new one, which prevents **stack overflow** and reduces the overhead of recursive calls.

Example: Tail Recursion for Factorial

To convert the factorial function into a tail-recursive version, we can pass the result as an argument to the recursive call. This eliminates the need for additional function calls after the recursive step.

python

```python
def factorial_tail(n, accumulator=1):
```

```
if n == 0:
    return accumulator
else:
    return factorial_tail(n - 1, n *
accumulator)


# Using the tail-recursive version
result = factorial_tail(5)  # Output: 120
```

In the tail-recursive version, `accumulator` holds the intermediate result, and there's no need to return after the recursive call—thus enabling the function to be optimized for performance.

3. Memoization

Memoization is a technique used to optimize recursive algorithms by storing the results of expensive function calls and reusing them when the same inputs occur again. This eliminates redundant calculations and reduces the time complexity of certain algorithms.

Memoization is particularly useful for algorithms with overlapping subproblems, such as the **Fibonacci sequence**, where the same values are computed multiple times.

Example: Fibonacci Sequence with Memoization

Let's look at the recursive Fibonacci sequence algorithm and optimize it using memoization. The Fibonacci sequence is defined as:

```
fib(0) = 0

fib(1) = 1

fib(n) = fib(n-1) + fib(n-2) for n > 1
```

Naive recursion has exponential time complexity due to the repeated calculation of the same Fibonacci numbers. We can optimize this with memoization:

python

```python
# Memoization with a dictionary to store
previously computed results
def fibonacci(n, memo={}):
    if n in memo:
        return memo[n]
    if n <= 1:
        return n
    memo[n] = fibonacci(n - 1, memo) + fibonacci(n - 2, memo)
    return memo[n]

# Using the memoized version
result = fibonacci(10)  # Output: 55
```

In this example, the function stores previously calculated Fibonacci numbers in the memo dictionary. When the function encounters the same value of n again, it returns the result directly from memo, eliminating redundant calculations.

Example: Optimizing Recursive Fibonacci Sequence Generation

The **naive recursive Fibonacci** function can be inefficient because it recalculates Fibonacci numbers repeatedly. Let's compare the time complexities of the naive recursive Fibonacci function and the optimized version with memoization.

Naive Recursive Fibonacci:

python

```python
def fibonacci_naive(n):
    if n <= 1:
        return n
    return    fibonacci_naive(n    -    1)    +
fibonacci_naive(n - 2)
```

Time Complexity: $O(2^n)$

Space Complexity: $O(n)$ (due to the recursion stack)

Optimized Fibonacci with Memoization:

python

```
def fibonacci_memoized(n, memo={}):
    if n in memo:
        return memo[n]
    if n <= 1:
        return n
    memo[n] = fibonacci_memoized(n - 1, memo) +
fibonacci_memoized(n - 2, memo)
    return memo[n]
```

Time Complexity: O(n) (due to memoization)

Space Complexity: O(n) (for the memo dictionary)

As you can see, memoization significantly reduces the time complexity of the Fibonacci sequence generation, from O(2^n) to O(n), by avoiding the redundant recalculation of Fibonacci numbers.

Real-World Example: Optimizing Recursion in Factorial Calculations

Let's say you are working on a system that requires frequent factorial calculations, and the input numbers can be large. The recursive approach without optimization can lead to stack overflow or performance degradation due to the deep recursion. You can optimize this by using tail recursion or by implementing memoization to avoid recalculating the same factorials.

Naive Recursive Factorial:

python

```python
def factorial_naive(n):
    if n == 0:
        return 1
    return n * factorial_naive(n - 1)
```

For large n, the above function can cause stack overflow or significant performance degradation due to its deep recursive calls.

Optimized Factorial Using Tail Recursion:

python

```python
def factorial_tail(n, accumulator=1):
    if n == 0:
        return accumulator
    return factorial_tail(n - 1, n * accumulator)

# Tail recursion avoids excessive stack usage
print(factorial_tail(1000))  # More efficient for
large values
```

In this example, the tail-recursive version avoids additional function calls after recursion, allowing Python to optimize the recursion stack.

Conclusion

In this chapter, we discussed **recursion** and **iteration**, and we explored the benefits and limitations of both approaches. We also covered optimization techniques for recursive algorithms, including **tail recursion optimization** and **memoization**, to improve both time and space efficiency. We used the **Fibonacci sequence** as a practical example to demonstrate how memoization can significantly optimize performance.

By understanding when to use recursion and how to optimize recursive algorithms, you can write more efficient code and avoid common pitfalls like excessive recursion depth or redundant computations. In the following chapters, we will continue to explore more advanced optimization strategies for various types of algorithms.

CHAPTER 7

DYNAMIC PROGRAMMING: BREAKING DOWN COMPLEX PROBLEMS

Dynamic programming (DP) is a powerful technique for solving problems that involve making decisions over time and optimizing an objective. Many complex problems in computer science, particularly those related to optimization and resource allocation, can be solved more efficiently using dynamic programming. This chapter will introduce you to the concept of dynamic programming, explain its core principles, and show how it can be applied to solve real-world problems like the **knapsack problem** and the **shortest path** problem.

Introduction to Dynamic Programming

Dynamic programming is an algorithm design paradigm that solves problems by breaking them down into smaller subproblems, solving each subproblem only once, and storing the results of these subproblems (often referred to as "memoization") to avoid redundant calculations. This is especially useful when the problem involves overlapping subproblems.

Dynamic programming can be thought of as an **optimization technique** that saves time by storing previously computed results, which allows us to avoid recalculating them.

Key Characteristics of Dynamic Programming:

Optimal Substructure: The problem can be broken down into smaller subproblems that can be solved independently. The solution to the problem is built from the solutions to its subproblems.

Overlapping Subproblems: The problem can be broken down into subproblems that are solved multiple times during the execution of the algorithm. Storing the results of these subproblems avoids recomputation.

When both of these characteristics are present, dynamic programming can be applied to efficiently solve the problem.

The Importance of Memoization and Tabulation

Memoization and tabulation are the two primary techniques used to implement dynamic programming solutions.

1. Memoization (Top-Down Approach)

Memoization is a **top-down** approach where the problem is solved recursively, but intermediate results (subproblem solutions) are stored, so they aren't recomputed. It is implemented using a **recursion** structure and a data structure (usually an array, dictionary, or hash map) to store the computed values.

How It Works:

Solve the problem recursively.

Store the results of subproblems in a table (usually a dictionary or list).

Before solving a subproblem, check if the result is already in the table. If it is, return it; otherwise, compute it and store it.

Example: Fibonacci Sequence with Memoization

python

```python
def fibonacci(n, memo={}):
    if n in memo:
        return memo[n]
    if n <= 1:
        return n
    memo[n]  =  fibonacci(n  -  1,  memo)  +
fibonacci(n - 2, memo)
    return memo[n]


# Calculate the 10th Fibonacci number
```

77

```
result = fibonacci(10)
print(result)   # Output: 55
```

In this example, the Fibonacci numbers are computed recursively, and previously computed values are stored in the `memo` dictionary to avoid redundant calculations.

2. Tabulation (Bottom-Up Approach)

Tabulation is a **bottom-up** approach where we solve the problem by filling up a table (usually an array) iteratively, starting from the smallest subproblems and working towards the larger problem.

How It Works:

> Start by solving the smallest subproblems (usually with a base case).

> Use previously computed values to fill the table for larger subproblems, until you reach the solution to the original problem.

Tabulation generally has a lower space overhead than memoization because it avoids the recursion stack. It is often more efficient in terms of both time and space when the solution can be constructed iteratively.

Example: Fibonacci Sequence with Tabulation

78

python

```python
def fibonacci(n):
    if n <= 1:
        return n
    table = [0] * (n + 1)
    table[1] = 1
    for i in range(2, n + 1):
        table[i] = table[i - 1] + table[i - 2]
    return table[n]

# Calculate the 10th Fibonacci number
result = fibonacci(10)
print(result)   # Output: 55
```

In this example, the Fibonacci sequence is computed iteratively using a table to store intermediate results.

Solving Common Dynamic Programming Problems Efficiently

Dynamic programming is especially useful for optimization problems. Let's explore a couple of common problems that are often solved using dynamic programming: the **knapsack problem** and the **shortest path** problem.

1. Knapsack Problem

The **0/1 knapsack problem** involves a set of items, each with a weight and a value, and a knapsack with a limited weight capacity.

The goal is to find the maximum value that can be obtained by selecting a subset of items such that the total weight does not exceed the knapsack's capacity.

The problem is formulated as follows:

Given n items, each with a weight w[i] and value v[i].

Given a knapsack with capacity W.

Maximize the total value V subject to the constraint that the total weight W does not exceed the capacity.

Dynamic Programming Solution (Tabulation):

python

```python
def knapsack(weights, values, capacity):
    n = len(weights)
    dp = [[0] * (capacity + 1) for _ in range(n
+ 1)]

    for i in range(n + 1):
        for w in range(capacity + 1):
            if i == 0 or w == 0:
                dp[i][w] = 0
            elif weights[i-1] <= w:
                dp[i][w]  =   max(values[i-1]   +
dp[i-1][w - weights[i-1]], dp[i-1][w])
```

```
        else:
            dp[i][w] = dp[i-1][w]

    return dp[n][capacity]

# Example usage:
weights = [2, 3, 4, 5]
values = [3, 4, 5, 6]
capacity = 5
result = knapsack(weights, values, capacity)
print(result)   # Output: 7
```

In this solution, the table dp[i][w] stores the maximum value that can be obtained with the first i items and a knapsack capacity w. The algorithm fills in the table from the smallest subproblems (base cases) to the final solution.

2. Shortest Path Problem (Dijkstra's Algorithm)

In graph theory, the **shortest path problem** involves finding the shortest path between two nodes in a graph. A well-known algorithm to solve this problem is **Dijkstra's Algorithm**, which uses dynamic programming to find the shortest path in a weighted graph.

Dynamic Programming Solution (Dijkstra's Algorithm):

python

```
import heapq

def dijkstra(graph, start):
    # Priority queue to store (distance, vertex)
pairs
    pq = [(0, start)]
    distances = {start: 0}

    while pq:
        current_distance, current_vertex =
heapq.heappop(pq)

        # Skip processing if we have already
found a shorter path
        if current_distance >
distances.get(current_vertex, float('inf')):
            continue

        # Explore each neighbor of the current
vertex
        for neighbor, weight in
graph[current_vertex].items():
            distance = current_distance + weight
            if distance <
distances.get(neighbor, float('inf')):
                distances[neighbor] = distance
                heapq.heappush(pq, (distance,
neighbor))
```

```
    return distances

# Example graph (adjacency list representation)
graph = {
    'A': {'B': 1, 'C': 4},
    'B': {'A': 1, 'C': 2, 'D': 5},
    'C': {'A': 4, 'B': 2, 'D': 1},
    'D': {'B': 5, 'C': 1}
}


# Find the shortest paths from vertex 'A'
result = dijkstra(graph, 'A')
print(result)  # Output: {'A': 0, 'B': 1, 'C': 3,
'D': 4}
```

Dijkstra's algorithm iteratively explores the shortest path to each node by maintaining a priority queue of nodes to explore and updating the shortest path as it goes. It's an efficient way to solve the shortest path problem, with a time complexity of $O(E \log V)$, where E is the number of edges and V is the number of vertices.

Real-World Examples: Optimization of the Knapsack Problem, Shortest Path

Optimization of the Knapsack Problem: The knapsack problem is commonly encountered in logistics, finance, and resource allocation. For example, a logistics company might use the knapsack problem to determine the most valuable cargo to load into a limited-capacity truck, ensuring the highest value per weight unit. By applying dynamic programming, the problem can be solved efficiently even for large datasets.

Optimization of the Shortest Path (Routing): The shortest path problem is central to applications in networking, transportation, and map services. For instance, a GPS application uses Dijkstra's algorithm to find the shortest route between two locations. The efficiency of this algorithm ensures that real-time traffic conditions and detours are accounted for when computing the best path.

Conclusion

In this chapter, we introduced **dynamic programming (DP)** and explored its fundamental principles: **optimal substructure** and **overlapping subproblems**. We discussed how to implement dynamic programming using two main approaches: **memoization (top-down)** and **tabulation (bottom-up)**. We also examined real-world applications, including the **knapsack problem** and **shortest path algorithms**, which benefit from DP optimization.

Dynamic programming is an essential technique for solving complex problems efficiently, especially those that involve optimization. By breaking problems down into smaller subproblems and storing the results, we can avoid redundant computations and achieve faster, more efficient algorithms. In the next chapters, we'll continue exploring additional advanced optimization strategies.

CHAPTER 8

GREEDY ALGORITHMS: MAKING OPTIMAL LOCAL CHOICES

Greedy algorithms are a class of algorithms that solve problems by making a sequence of choices, each of which looks the best at the current step, without worrying about the future consequences. The idea behind greedy algorithms is to take the most immediate, "greedy" option, hoping that this local optimum will lead to a globally optimal solution.

In this chapter, we will:

Understand the **greedy approach** to problem-solving.

Analyze when greedy algorithms work optimally.

Explore an **example of a greedy algorithm** for the **fractional knapsack problem**.

Discuss how to **optimize greedy algorithms for time efficiency**.

Understanding the Greedy Approach to Problem-Solving

A **greedy algorithm** makes a series of choices, each of which is the best option at that moment, without considering the larger picture or future consequences. The core idea is to take the best choice available at each step and hope that these choices will lead to a globally optimal solution.

Key Characteristics of Greedy Algorithms:

Local Optimality: At each step, the algorithm makes a decision that seems the best at the current moment.

Irrevocable Decisions: Once a choice is made, it is not revisited. The algorithm does not backtrack or reconsider its decisions.

No Look-Ahead: Greedy algorithms do not anticipate the consequences of their choices in the future, making them inherently myopic.

For example, when selecting items to maximize profit, a greedy algorithm might pick the highest-profit item available, then move on to the next highest-profit item, continuing this process until all resources (e.g., capacity) are used up.

When Do Greedy Algorithms Work?

A greedy algorithm works optimally (i.e., it yields the best possible solution) when:

Greedy Choice Property: A global optimum can be arrived at by selecting the local optimum at each step. That is, making the best decision at each step leads to the best overall solution.

Optimal Substructure: The problem can be broken down into subproblems, and the solution to these subproblems can be combined to form the global optimum.

In cases where these two properties are satisfied, a greedy approach will provide an optimal solution.

When Do Greedy Algorithms Not Work?

Greedy algorithms are not guaranteed to work optimally for all problems. In some cases, choosing the local optimum may not lead to the global optimum. Problems that do not have the greedy choice property or optimal substructure typically require other techniques like **dynamic programming** or **backtracking**.

Analyzing When Greedy Algorithms Work Optimally

To determine whether a greedy algorithm will provide an optimal solution, it's essential to verify if the problem satisfies the greedy choice property and optimal substructure.

Example: The Fractional Knapsack Problem

In the **fractional knapsack problem**, you are given a set of items, each with a weight and a value, and a knapsack with a fixed capacity. The goal is to maximize the value of the items in the knapsack, where you can take fractions of items (as opposed to the 0/1 knapsack problem where you can only take the entire item).

The greedy approach works optimally for this problem because:

> **Greedy Choice Property**: At each step, we can choose the item with the highest value-to-weight ratio to maximize the total value of the knapsack.

> **Optimal Substructure**: The problem can be divided into smaller subproblems, where at each stage we take the item with the best value-to-weight ratio, leading to the global optimum.

Example: Greedy Algorithm for the Fractional Knapsack Problem

Here's a step-by-step implementation of a greedy algorithm to solve the fractional knapsack problem:

Problem: Given a set of items, each with a value and weight, and a knapsack with a fixed capacity, determine the maximum value we can achieve by filling the knapsack (with the option to take fractional parts of the items).

python

```python
# Define the Item class to store the value,
weight, and value-to-weight ratio
class Item:
    def __init__(self, value, weight):
        self.value = value
        self.weight = weight
        self.ratio = value / weight  # Value-to-
weight ratio


# Greedy Knapsack Algorithm
def fractional_knapsack(capacity, items):
    # Sort items by value-to-weight ratio in
descending order
    items.sort(key=lambda    x:    x.ratio,
reverse=True)

    total_value = 0
```

90

```
    for item in items:
        if capacity == 0:
            break  # Knapsack is full

        # If the item can fully fit, take it
        if item.weight <= capacity:
            total_value += item.value
            capacity -= item.weight
        else:
            # If only part of the item fits, take
the fraction of it
            total_value    +=    item.value    *
(capacity / item.weight)
            break  # Knapsack is full

    return total_value

# Example usage:
items = [Item(60, 10), Item(100, 20), Item(120,
30)]
capacity = 50
max_value = fractional_knapsack(capacity, items)
print(f"Maximum value in Knapsack: {max_value}")
# Output: 240.0
```

In this example:

The **items** are first sorted by their value-to-weight ratio
(higher ratios are prioritized).

91

The algorithm then proceeds to fill the knapsack by taking as much of the item as possible, prioritizing the highest value-to-weight ratio.

The algorithm maximizes the value by considering fractions of items when the knapsack is not full.

Time Complexity:

Sorting the items takes O(n log n), where n is the number of items.

The iteration to fill the knapsack takes O(n) in the worst case.

Therefore, the time complexity is O(n log n).

Optimizing Greedy Algorithms for Time Efficiency

Greedy algorithms can often be optimized for better time efficiency, especially when combined with techniques like sorting or using efficient data structures. Here are some strategies to optimize greedy algorithms:

Efficient Sorting: Many greedy algorithms (like the fractional knapsack problem) require sorting the elements (e.g., by value-to-weight ratio). Optimizing the sorting step is crucial for time efficiency. Using algorithms like

QuickSort or **MergeSort** (with time complexity O(n log n)) can reduce the sorting overhead.

Data Structures: Choosing the right data structure can improve the performance of greedy algorithms:

> **Priority Queues (Heaps)**: For problems where you need to repeatedly choose the "best" option (e.g., Dijkstra's algorithm for shortest path), using a **min-heap** or **max-heap** allows you to efficiently select the next best option in O(log n) time.

> **Hashing**: In problems involving fast lookups, such as certain graph algorithms, hashing can optimize the process of finding or updating values.

Greedy Choice Preprocessing: In some cases, you can preprocess the data to reduce the complexity of the greedy choice step. For instance, if you're solving a scheduling problem, you might preprocess the tasks by sorting them based on their duration or priority before applying a greedy approach.

Real-World Examples: Optimization of the Knapsack Problem, Shortest Path

Knapsack Problem:

Logistics and Packing: The fractional knapsack problem models real-world scenarios where resources (e.g., space in a container) need to be allocated to maximize value. This is common in logistics, where you want to maximize the value of items loaded into a truck with a limited capacity.

Investment Portfolio: The problem can also be applied to investment portfolios, where an investor needs to choose a mix of assets (e.g., stocks, bonds) with the goal of maximizing returns while staying within a budget (capacity).

Shortest Path (Greedy for Dijkstra's Algorithm):

Navigation and Routing: Greedy algorithms like **Dijkstra's algorithm** are widely used in real-time navigation systems (e.g., Google Maps, GPS devices) to find the shortest path between locations on a map. The greedy approach ensures that at each step, the algorithm selects the shortest known path to a destination, updating the path as new routes are discovered.

Network Routing: In computer networks, routing protocols like OSPF (Open Shortest Path First) use greedy algorithms to determine the shortest path between routers, ensuring efficient data transmission with minimal latency.

Conclusion

In this chapter, we explored **greedy algorithms**—a class of algorithms that make local optimal choices at each step to solve complex problems. We discussed the key principles behind greedy algorithms, when they are effective, and when they may not work. Using the **fractional knapsack problem** as an example, we saw how a greedy algorithm can efficiently solve optimization problems by choosing items with the highest value-to-weight ratio.

We also looked at how to **optimize greedy algorithms** for time efficiency by using sorting, efficient data structures (like heaps), and preprocessing. Greedy algorithms are highly effective in solving certain types of problems, especially those involving resource allocation, pathfinding, and scheduling. Understanding when and how to apply these algorithms is crucial for optimizing performance in real-world applications.

CHAPTER 9

DIVIDE AND CONQUER: OPTIMIZING RECURSIVE STRATEGIES

The **divide and conquer** strategy is one of the most powerful algorithm design paradigms. It breaks down complex problems into smaller, more manageable subproblems, solves each subproblem independently, and combines their results to solve the original problem. This approach is used extensively in both theoretical and practical algorithm design, and it can lead to significant improvements in both time and space efficiency.

In this chapter, we will explore:

Explanation of the divide and conquer strategy.

How to efficiently solve problems using divide and conquer.

Examples of optimizing sorting algorithms (merge sort and quicksort) using divide and conquer.

Practical use cases of divide and conquer in real-world systems.

Explanation of Divide and Conquer Strategy

The divide and conquer approach involves three main steps:

Divide: Break the problem into smaller, non-overlapping subproblems.

Conquer: Solve each subproblem recursively.

Combine: Combine the solutions of the subproblems to form the solution to the original problem.

This strategy is particularly effective when the subproblems are similar to the original problem but smaller in size. By solving smaller subproblems, divide and conquer can often reduce the overall complexity of the problem.

Key Characteristics of Divide and Conquer:

Recursive Decomposition: The problem is broken down into subproblems that are easier to handle.

Independence of Subproblems: The subproblems are solved independently, making parallelization easier in some cases.

Combination Step: After solving the subproblems, their results are combined to form the final solution.

Efficiently Solving Problems Using Divide and Conquer

Divide and conquer is particularly effective for problems that can be divided into smaller, self-similar subproblems. The most common example of this is sorting, where an array is split into smaller subarrays, each of which is sorted independently and then merged to form the sorted array.

Key Advantages:

Improved Time Complexity: By dividing a problem into smaller parts, divide and conquer often reduces the time complexity. For example, merge sort and quicksort use divide and conquer to achieve $O(n \log n)$ time complexity, which is much better than the $O(n^2)$ time complexity of simpler algorithms like bubble sort.

Parallelism: Divide and conquer algorithms are inherently parallelizable, meaning that independent subproblems can be solved simultaneously, leading to potential performance gains on multi-core processors.

Space Efficiency: Some divide and conquer algorithms (like quicksort) operate in place, meaning that they do not require additional memory for recursion, while others (like merge sort) may require extra space.

Example: Optimizing Merge Sort and Quick Sort Using Divide and Conquer

Let's look at two well-known sorting algorithms that use the divide and conquer strategy: **merge sort** and **quicksort**.

1. Merge Sort

Merge Sort is a stable, comparison-based sorting algorithm that divides the array into two halves, recursively sorts each half, and then merges the sorted halves back together.

Steps of Merge Sort:

Divide: Split the array into two halves.

Conquer: Recursively sort each half.

Combine: Merge the two sorted halves into a single sorted array.

Merge Sort Implementation:

python

```python
def merge_sort(arr):
    if len(arr) > 1:
        mid = len(arr) // 2
        left_half = arr[:mid]
```

99

```python
    right_half = arr[mid:]

    # Recursively sort both halves
    merge_sort(left_half)
    merge_sort(right_half)

    i = j = k = 0

    # Merge the sorted halves
    while i < len(left_half) and j < len(right_half):
        if left_half[i] < right_half[j]:
            arr[k] = left_half[i]
            i += 1
        else:
            arr[k] = right_half[j]
            j += 1
        k += 1

    # If any elements are left in the left half, add them
    while i < len(left_half):
        arr[k] = left_half[i]
        i += 1
        k += 1

    # If any elements are left in the right half, add them
    while j < len(right_half):
```

100

```
        arr[k] = right_half[j]
        j += 1
        k += 1

# Example usage
arr = [38, 27, 43, 3, 9, 82, 10]
merge_sort(arr)
print("Sorted array:", arr)
```

Time Complexity: O(n log n) (n is the number of elements, log n is the number of levels of recursion)

Space Complexity: O(n) (for storing the left and right halves during the merge step)

2. Quick Sort

Quick Sort is an efficient, comparison-based sorting algorithm that works by selecting a "pivot" element, partitioning the array into elements less than the pivot and elements greater than the pivot, and then recursively sorting the two partitions.

Steps of Quick Sort:

Divide: Select a pivot element and partition the array into two subarrays: one with elements less than the pivot and the other with elements greater than the pivot.

Conquer: Recursively sort each subarray.

101

Combine: After sorting, the array is combined by placing the pivot in its correct position.

Quick Sort Implementation:

python

```python
def quick_sort(arr):
    if len(arr) <= 1:
        return arr
    pivot = arr[len(arr) // 2]   # Choose the
middle element as pivot
    left = [x for x in arr if x < pivot]
    middle = [x for x in arr if x == pivot]
    right = [x for x in arr if x > pivot]
    return    quick_sort(left)    +    middle    +
quick_sort(right)

# Example usage
arr = [38, 27, 43, 3, 9, 82, 10]
sorted_arr = quick_sort(arr)
print("Sorted array:", sorted_arr)
```

Time Complexity:

Best and Average Case: $O(n \log n)$ (when the pivot is chosen well)

Worst Case: $O(n^2)$ (when the pivot is poorly chosen)

Space Complexity: O(log n) (due to the recursion stack)

Comparison of Merge Sort and Quick Sort

Merge Sort guarantees O(n log n) time complexity in all cases but requires additional space for the temporary arrays during the merge step.

Quick Sort has a best-case time complexity of O(n log n), but its worst-case time complexity can degrade to $O(n^2)$ if the pivot selection is poor. However, it is often faster in practice due to smaller constant factors, and it sorts in place without requiring extra space.

Practical Use Cases for Divide and Conquer in Real-World Systems

Divide and conquer is not limited to sorting algorithms; it can be applied to a wide variety of problems across different domains. Here are some real-world use cases where divide and conquer is particularly effective:

Parallel Processing: Divide and conquer algorithms are inherently parallelizable, meaning that different subproblems can be solved simultaneously on different processors. For example, **parallel merge sort** and **parallel quicksort** can be implemented to take advantage of multiple CPU cores, significantly speeding up the sorting process.

Matrix Multiplication: Matrix multiplication is a fundamental operation in many scientific and engineering applications. The **Strassen algorithm** for matrix multiplication uses divide and conquer to multiply matrices in $O(n^{2.81})$ time, which is more efficient than the standard $O(n^3)$ matrix multiplication algorithm. This technique is widely used in high-performance computing.

Fast Fourier Transform (FFT): The **Fast Fourier Transform** is a divide and conquer algorithm used in signal processing, data compression, and image processing. The FFT algorithm decomposes a Fourier transform into smaller Fourier transforms, reducing its time complexity from $O(n^2)$ to $O(n \log n)$, which is a significant improvement in performance for large datasets.

Binary Search: Binary search is a classic example of divide and conquer. It efficiently finds an element in a sorted array by repeatedly dividing the search space in half, making it very effective for search problems in databases and file systems.

Computer Graphics: Divide and conquer techniques are used in rendering algorithms, such as **quicksort** for sorting 3D objects in a scene. In graphics, divide and conquer is also used in algorithms like **ray tracing** for

104

simulating the paths of light through a scene, breaking down complex scenes into smaller subproblems.

Closest Pair of Points: The closest pair of points problem involves finding the two points in a plane that are closest to each other. This problem is commonly used in computational geometry and applications like geographical data analysis. The **divide and conquer approach** reduces the time complexity of the naive algorithm from $O(n^2)$ to $O(n \log n)$.

Conclusion

In this chapter, we explored the **divide and conquer strategy**, a powerful technique for solving complex problems by breaking them down into simpler subproblems. We learned that divide and conquer is widely used in algorithms like **merge sort** and **quicksort**, both of which optimize recursive strategies by dividing the problem into smaller parts and combining the results efficiently. We also discussed the real-world applicability of divide and conquer, including in **parallel processing**, **matrix multiplication**, **FFT**, and more.

By leveraging divide and conquer, we can significantly improve the performance of algorithms, especially for large datasets or problems that can be decomposed into independent subproblems.

This technique is a fundamental tool for efficient algorithm design and optimization.

CHAPTER 10

GRAPH ALGORITHMS AND THEIR OPTIMIZATIONS

Graph algorithms are foundational to many areas in computer science, including networking, routing, social network analysis, and artificial intelligence. They deal with problems related to **graphs**, which consist of vertices (nodes) and edges (connections between nodes). In this chapter, we will explore several key graph algorithms, how to optimize them for better performance, and some real-world examples where these optimizations are essential.

This chapter will cover:

Introduction to Graph Algorithms (DFS, BFS, Dijkstra's algorithm)

Optimizing Graph Algorithms for Performance

Use Cases: Shortest Path and Network Optimization

Real-World Examples of Graph Algorithm Optimizations

Introduction to Graph Algorithms

Graph algorithms are used to solve problems that involve traversing, searching, or optimizing on graphs. Here are a few key algorithms that are commonly used:

1. Depth-First Search (DFS)

DFS is a graph traversal algorithm that starts at a source node and explores as far as possible along each branch before backtracking. It uses a **stack** (either implicitly through recursion or explicitly) to keep track of vertices to visit.

> **Time Complexity**: O(V + E), where V is the number of vertices and E is the number of edges in the graph.

> **Space Complexity**: O(V) (for the recursion stack in the worst case).

DFS is particularly useful for tasks like:

> **Topological sorting** of directed acyclic graphs (DAGs).

> **Cycle detection** in graphs.

> **Pathfinding** when all paths need to be explored.

Example of DFS:

python

```python
def dfs(graph, start, visited=None):
    if visited is None:
        visited = set()
    visited.add(start)
    for neighbor in graph[start]:
        if neighbor not in visited:
            dfs(graph, neighbor, visited)
    return visited

# Example graph (adjacency list)
graph = {
    'A': ['B', 'C'],
    'B': ['A', 'D', 'E'],
    'C': ['A', 'F'],
    'D': ['B'],
    'E': ['B', 'F'],
    'F': ['C', 'E']
}
print(dfs(graph, 'A'))  # Output: {'A', 'B', 'C',
'D', 'E', 'F'}
```

2. Breadth-First Search (BFS)

BFS is another graph traversal algorithm that explores all the neighbors of a vertex before moving on to the next level of neighbors. BFS uses a **queue** to keep track of the nodes to visit next.

Time Complexity: O(V + E), similar to DFS.

Space Complexity: O(V) (for the queue).

BFS is ideal for:

Finding the **shortest path** in an unweighted graph.

Level-order traversal in trees or graphs.

Connected components in an undirected graph.

Example of BFS:

python

```python
from collections import deque

def bfs(graph, start):
    visited = set()
    queue = deque([start])
    visited.add(start)

    while queue:
        vertex = queue.popleft()
        print(vertex, end=" ")
        for neighbor in graph[vertex]:
            if neighbor not in visited:
                visited.add(neighbor)
                queue.append(neighbor)
```

```
# Example graph (adjacency list)
graph = {
    'A': ['B', 'C'],
    'B': ['A', 'D', 'E'],
    'C': ['A', 'F'],
    'D': ['B'],
    'E': ['B', 'F'],
    'F': ['C', 'E']
}
bfs(graph, 'A')  # Output: A B C D E F
```

3. Dijkstra's Algorithm

Dijkstra's algorithm is a well-known algorithm used for finding the shortest path from a source vertex to all other vertices in a **weighted graph** with **non-negative edge weights**. It works by iteratively selecting the vertex with the smallest tentative distance, updating the tentative distances of its neighbors, and then repeating the process until all vertices are visited.

Time Complexity:

Using a simple array or list for priority queue: $O(V^2)$

Using a binary heap (priority queue): $O((V + E) \log V)$

Space Complexity: $O(V)$ for storing the distances and visited vertices.

111

Example of Dijkstra's Algorithm:

python

```python
import heapq

def dijkstra(graph, start):
    # Priority queue (min-heap) for choosing the vertex with the smallest tentative distance
    pq = [(0, start)]
    distances = {start: 0}
    while pq:
        current_distance, current_vertex = heapq.heappop(pq)

        if current_distance > distances.get(current_vertex, float('inf')):
            continue

        for neighbor, weight in graph[current_vertex]:
            distance = current_distance + weight
            if distance < distances.get(neighbor, float('inf')):
                distances[neighbor] = distance
                heapq.heappush(pq, (distance, neighbor))

    return distances
```

```
# Example graph (adjacency list with weights)
graph = {
    'A': [('B', 1), ('C', 4)],
    'B': [('A', 1), ('C', 2), ('D', 5)],
    'C': [('A', 4), ('B', 2), ('D', 1)],
    'D': [('B', 5), ('C', 1)]
}
print(dijkstra(graph, 'A'))   # Output: {'A': 0,
'B': 1, 'C': 3, 'D': 4}
```

Optimizing Graph Algorithms for Performance

While graph algorithms like DFS, BFS, and Dijkstra's algorithm are efficient in general, their performance can be further optimized depending on the specific problem and constraints. Here are several strategies for improving the performance of graph algorithms:

1. Optimizing BFS/DFS with Early Stopping

In some applications, BFS and DFS don't need to explore the entire graph. Early stopping can be used when:

The target node is found: In a search problem, if the target is found, the algorithm can terminate immediately.

Certain conditions are met: For instance, in DFS, if a path exceeds a certain depth or length, we can stop further exploration to avoid unnecessary computations.

2. Using a Priority Queue for Dijkstra's Algorithm

Dijkstra's algorithm can be significantly optimized by using a **priority queue (min-heap)** instead of a simple array. This allows for faster updates of the minimum tentative distance, reducing the time complexity from $O(V^2)$ to $O((V + E) \log V)$, especially when the graph is sparse.

3. *Using A Algorithm for Shortest Path**

If additional information about the problem is available, the *A algorithm** can be used as an optimized version of Dijkstra's algorithm. It uses a heuristic to guide the search, reducing the number of nodes explored and improving efficiency, especially in problems like navigation or route planning.

4. Graph Sparsity

In very large graphs, sparse graphs (with fewer edges compared to the number of vertices) are common. Many graph algorithms can be optimized by:

> **Using adjacency lists**: Instead of using an adjacency matrix, which takes $O(V^2)$ space, an adjacency list only stores the edges for each vertex, saving space and time for sparse graphs.

Edge pruning: Removing redundant or unnecessary edges, especially in the case of undirected graphs or graphs with high edge density.

Use Cases: Shortest Path and Network Optimization

Graph algorithms have numerous real-world applications, particularly in **network optimization, routing**, and **pathfinding**. Here are some practical use cases:

1. Shortest Path in Navigation Systems

In GPS navigation systems, Dijkstra's algorithm or A* is used to find the shortest path between two points on a map. These systems rely on a graph where intersections are vertices and roads are edges. Real-time updates like traffic conditions or road closures are incorporated into the graph to dynamically adjust the shortest path.

Optimization: By using **A*** or **Dijkstra's algorithm** with dynamic adjustments, GPS systems provide optimal routes based on real-time data.

2. Network Routing (Internet and Communication)

Graph algorithms are used in **network routing** to determine the best path for data packets to travel across a network of routers. For instance, the **Open Shortest Path First (OSPF)** routing protocol uses Dijkstra's algorithm to determine the shortest path for data to travel through a network.

> **Optimization**: With the right data structures (such as priority queues) and optimized algorithms, these routing algorithms can handle massive networks efficiently.

3. Social Network Analysis

In social network analysis, nodes represent people, and edges represent relationships. Algorithms like DFS, BFS, and others can be used to find **strongly connected components**, detect **cycles**, or identify **communities** in a network. Understanding the structure of social networks can help in areas such as recommendation systems, viral marketing, or detecting fraud.

4. Supply Chain and Logistics Optimization

In logistics and supply chain management, graphs can represent delivery routes, warehouses, and delivery times. Shortest path algorithms help find the most efficient delivery routes, saving time and costs.

> **Optimization**: Graph algorithms can be enhanced with real-time data, allowing systems to dynamically adjust routes based on traffic, delays, or other factors.

Real-World Examples of Graph Algorithm Optimizations

Google Maps: Google Maps uses Dijkstra's algorithm or A* to provide real-time traffic-aware navigation. Optimizing these algorithms allows Google Maps to compute the best routes in real time, factoring in dynamic data such as traffic, road closures, and accidents.

Telecommunications: In telecommunications, **network optimization** algorithms like Dijkstra's algorithm are used to route calls or data packets through a network, ensuring that resources are used efficiently and traffic congestion is minimized.

Game Development: In many video games, graph algorithms are used to find the shortest path between two points (e.g., moving characters or NPCs) or to calculate the most efficient way to solve puzzles or map traversals.

Recommendation Systems: In social media or e-commerce platforms, graph-based algorithms help make **recommendations** by identifying the shortest or most connected paths between users, items, or interests, optimizing how suggestions are made.

Conclusion

In this chapter, we explored several **graph algorithms** and their applications, including **DFS**, **BFS**, and **Dijkstra's algorithm**. We discussed optimization techniques for improving the performance of these algorithms, such as using **priority queues** for Dijkstra's algorithm, **early stopping** for BFS and DFS, and employing **A*** for more efficient shortest path search.

We also explored practical **use cases** of graph algorithms in real-world systems, from **navigation systems** to **network routing**, **social network analysis**, and **logistics optimization**.

Graph algorithms are crucial for solving a wide range of problems in computing, and their optimization is essential for handling large-scale, real-time applications efficiently.

CHAPTER 11

SEARCHING IN TREES AND GRAPHS

In this chapter, we will dive into searching in both **trees** and **graphs**, two fundamental data structures in computer science. We'll explore **tree traversal techniques**, how to **optimize tree search algorithms**, and strategies for **optimizing graph traversal**. These techniques are crucial for efficiently searching and manipulating hierarchical or interconnected data.

We will cover:

Tree traversal techniques (pre-order, in-order, post-order)

Optimizing tree search algorithms (e.g., AVL, Red-Black trees)

Balancing search trees for faster lookups

How to optimize graph traversal algorithms

Tree Traversal Techniques and Their Complexities

A **tree** is a hierarchical data structure consisting of nodes, where each node has a value and references to child nodes. **Tree**

119

traversal refers to the process of visiting all the nodes in a tree. There are three primary ways to traverse a binary tree:

1. Pre-order Traversal

In **pre-order traversal**, the algorithm visits the root node first, then recursively visits the left subtree and the right subtree.

> **Order**: Root → Left → Right

> **Time Complexity**: O(n), where n is the number of nodes in the tree.

> **Space Complexity**: O(h), where h is the height of the tree (due to the recursion stack).

Example:

python

```python
def pre_order(node):
    if node:
        print(node.value, end=" ")
        pre_order(node.left)
        pre_order(node.right)
```

2. In-order Traversal

In **in-order traversal**, the algorithm recursively visits the left subtree first, then the root node, and finally the right subtree. This

120

traversal is commonly used to visit nodes in **sorted order** in binary search trees (BST).

Order: Left → Root → Right

Time Complexity: O(n)

Space Complexity: O(h)

Example:

python

```
def in_order(node):
    if node:
        in_order(node.left)
        print(node.value, end=" ")
        in_order(node.right)
```

3. Post-order Traversal

In **post-order traversal**, the algorithm recursively visits the left subtree, the right subtree, and then the root node. This is typically used for **deleting nodes** or calculating the height of a tree.

Order: Left → Right → Root

Time Complexity: O(n)

Space Complexity: O(h)

Example:

python

```python
def post_order(node):
    if node:
        post_order(node.left)
        post_order(node.right)
        print(node.value, end=" ")
```

Tree Traversal Summary

Traversal	Order	Time Complexity	Space Complexity
Pre-order	Root → Left → Right	O(n)	O(h)
In-order	Left → Root → Right	O(n)	O(h)
Post-order	Left → Right → Root	O(n)	O(h)

Where n is the number of nodes in the tree, and h is the height of the tree.

Optimizing Tree Search Algorithms (e.g., AVL, Red-Black Trees)

When performing searches, insertions, or deletions in a tree, the height of the tree plays a crucial role in determining the time complexity. If the tree is **unbalanced**, operations can degrade to O(n), where n is the number of nodes, making the tree behave like a linked list. This is where **self-balancing binary search trees** (BSTs) come in.

1. AVL Trees

AVL trees are a type of self-balancing binary search tree where the difference in height between the left and right subtrees (called the **balance factor**) of every node is at most 1. If the balance factor becomes greater than 1 or less than -1, rotations are performed to restore balance.

Time Complexity for search, insert, and delete: O(log n)

Space Complexity: O(n) for storing the tree nodes.

Example of Rotations:

Left Rotation: Performed when a right-heavy subtree needs balancing.

Right Rotation: Performed when a left-heavy subtree needs balancing.

Double Rotation: Performed when a subtree is unbalanced in both directions.

2. Red-Black Trees

A **Red-Black Tree** is another self-balancing binary search tree, with the additional constraint that each node is either red or black. The red-black tree maintains a balance by enforcing certain properties, such as ensuring that no two red nodes are adjacent and the path from any node to its descendant leaves contains the same number of black nodes.

Time Complexity for search, insert, and delete: O(log n)

Space Complexity: O(n)

Red-Black trees are simpler to implement than AVL trees and require fewer rotations, which can make them more efficient in practice for certain use cases.

Balancing Search Trees for Faster Lookups

Balancing a search tree, like converting an unbalanced binary search tree into an AVL or Red-Black tree, reduces the height of the tree and ensures that all operations (search, insert, delete) occur in O(log n) time. Balancing is done by performing **rotations**, as mentioned above, to ensure that the tree remains balanced during insertions and deletions.

In the worst-case scenario of an unbalanced tree, the search time complexity can degrade to O(n). By ensuring the tree is balanced, the height of the tree is kept to a minimum (logarithmic height), which optimizes search performance.

Example: Balancing Search Trees for Faster Lookups

Consider the following example of balancing a tree using **AVL** rotations:

python

```python
class AVLNode:
    def __init__(self, value):
        self.value = value
        self.left = None
        self.right = None
        self.height = 1  # Height of the node

def left_rotate(root):
    new_root = root.right
    root.right = new_root.left
    new_root.left = root
    root.height   =   max(get_height(root.left),
get_height(root.right)) + 1
    new_root.height                               =
max(get_height(new_root.left),
get_height(new_root.right)) + 1
    return new_root
```

```
def get_height(node):
    if not node:
        return 0
    return node.height

# Example of inserting and balancing the tree
will involve maintaining the balance factor
```

The balancing ensures that the tree remains efficient for searching and insertion, with time complexity O(log n) in the best and worst cases.

How to Optimize Graph Traversal Algorithms

Graph traversal algorithms, such as **DFS** and **BFS**, are essential for exploring graphs, whether they are representing networks, trees, or other structures. Optimization of graph traversal algorithms depends on several factors, including graph type (directed or undirected), graph density (sparse or dense), and whether the graph is weighted.

1. Optimizing DFS and BFS with Early Stopping

In many applications, such as **searching for a target node** or **finding a path**, DFS and BFS can be optimized with **early stopping**. If the target is found during the traversal, the algorithm can immediately stop and return the result, preventing unnecessary exploration of other parts of the graph.

2. Using Data Structures for Efficient Search

The **choice of data structure** can significantly improve the performance of graph traversal:

- **Adjacency Lists**: More efficient for sparse graphs, as they only store the vertices and edges that exist, reducing space complexity.

- **Adjacency Matrix**: Suitable for dense graphs but requires $O(n^2)$ space, which can be inefficient for sparse graphs.

- **Priority Queues**: Used in algorithms like **Dijkstra's** for efficiently selecting the next node to visit based on priority or distance.

3. Optimizing DFS with Iterative Approach

In DFS, recursion can be expensive in terms of memory usage due to the call stack, especially for large graphs. An **iterative DFS** using a stack instead of recursion can help reduce memory usage and avoid stack overflow errors for deep graphs.

Example of Iterative DFS:

python

```
def iterative_dfs(graph, start):
    visited = set()
    stack = [start]

    while stack:
        vertex = stack.pop()
        if vertex not in visited:
            visited.add(vertex)
            for neighbor in graph[vertex]:
                stack.append(neighbor)
    return visited

# Example graph (adjacency list)
graph = {
    'A': ['B', 'C'],
    'B': ['A', 'D', 'E'],
    'C': ['A', 'F'],
    'D': ['B'],
    'E': ['B', 'F'],
    'F': ['C', 'E']
}
print(iterative_dfs(graph, 'A'))  # Output: {'A',
'B', 'C', 'D', 'E', 'F'}
```

Conclusion

In this chapter, we explored **tree traversal techniques** like pre-order, in-order, and post-order traversal, and discussed how these techniques are used to traverse binary trees. We also examined

tree search optimizations using **AVL trees** and **Red-Black trees**, both of which are self-balancing binary search trees designed to maintain O(log n) time complexity for search operations.

We also discussed how to **optimize graph traversal algorithms**, including DFS and BFS, by implementing **early stopping** and using efficient data structures like **adjacency lists** and **priority queues**. These optimizations help improve both the **time complexity** and **space complexity** of graph traversal, ensuring more efficient exploration of large graphs.

Understanding these techniques is crucial for efficiently searching and manipulating hierarchical and interconnected data structures, whether you're working with databases, network routing, or AI systems.

CHAPTER 12

DIVIDE AND CONQUER FOR SORTING AND SEARCHING

The **divide and conquer** paradigm is one of the most powerful techniques in algorithm design, particularly for sorting and searching. By breaking a problem into smaller subproblems, solving those subproblems recursively, and combining their solutions, divide and conquer algorithms can achieve optimal or near-optimal performance in many scenarios.

In this chapter, we will:

> **Analyze** the use of divide and conquer in **sorting** and **searching** algorithms.

> Discuss how to **optimize merge sort** and **binary search** for real-world applications.

> Provide **practical tips** for using divide and conquer in **competitive programming**.

Detailed Analysis of Divide and Conquer in Sorting and Searching

The divide and conquer approach works exceptionally well for both sorting and searching problems, where the idea is to recursively break the problem down into smaller, more manageable pieces. Let's explore how this strategy applies to **sorting** and **searching**.

1. Divide and Conquer in Sorting

The most common divide and conquer algorithms for sorting are **Merge Sort** and **Quick Sort**. Both algorithms follow the same basic pattern:

Divide: Split the array or list into smaller subarrays.

Conquer: Sort the subarrays recursively.

Combine: Merge the sorted subarrays into a single sorted array.

Merge Sort

Merge Sort is a stable, comparison-based sorting algorithm that divides the array into two halves, sorts them recursively, and then merges them back together. The merge operation ensures that the final array is sorted.

Time Complexity: $O(n \log n)$, where n is the number of elements in the array.

Space Complexity: $O(n)$ (due to the temporary arrays created during the merge step).

131

Example of Merge Sort:

python

```python
def merge_sort(arr):
    if len(arr) > 1:
        mid = len(arr) // 2
        left_half = arr[:mid]
        right_half = arr[mid:]

        merge_sort(left_half)
        merge_sort(right_half)

        i = j = k = 0
        while i < len(left_half) and j < len(right_half):
            if left_half[i] < right_half[j]:
                arr[k] = left_half[i]
                i += 1
            else:
                arr[k] = right_half[j]
                j += 1
            k += 1

        while i < len(left_half):
            arr[k] = left_half[i]
            i += 1
            k += 1

        while j < len(right_half):
```

```
            arr[k] = right_half[j]
            j += 1
            k += 1
    return arr


# Example usage
arr = [38, 27, 43, 3, 9, 82, 10]
merge_sort(arr)
print(arr)  # Output: [3, 9, 10, 27, 38, 43, 82]
```

Quick Sort

Quick Sort is another divide and conquer algorithm that works by selecting a **pivot** element and partitioning the array into two subarrays: one with elements less than the pivot, and one with elements greater than the pivot. The pivot is then placed in its correct position, and the process is repeated on the subarrays.

Time Complexity:

Best and Average Case: O(n log n)

Worst Case: O(n²) (when the pivot selection is poor)

Space Complexity: O(log n) (due to recursion stack)

Example of Quick Sort:

```python
python
```

```
def quick_sort(arr):
    if len(arr) <= 1:
        return arr
    pivot = arr[len(arr) // 2]    # Choose the
middle element as pivot
    left = [x for x in arr if x < pivot]
    middle = [x for x in arr if x == pivot]
    right = [x for x in arr if x > pivot]
    return    quick_sort(left)    +    middle    +
quick_sort(right)

# Example usage
arr = [38, 27, 43, 3, 9, 82, 10]
sorted_arr = quick_sort(arr)
print(sorted_arr)    # Output: [3, 9, 10, 27, 38,
43, 82]
```

Comparison of Merge Sort and Quick Sort:

Merge Sort guarantees O(n log n) time complexity in all cases, making it more predictable.

Quick Sort can perform faster in practice due to smaller constant factors, but it can degrade to $O(n^2)$ if the pivot is not chosen well.

2. Divide and Conquer in Searching

Divide and conquer also applies to searching, particularly when searching in **sorted arrays** or **search trees**. One of the most common divide and conquer algorithms for searching is **binary search**.

Binary Search

Binary Search works by repeatedly dividing a sorted array in half and checking whether the target element is in the left or right half. This process is repeated until the element is found or the search space is empty.

Time Complexity: O(log n), where n is the number of elements in the array.

Space Complexity: O(1) for iterative implementation, O(log n) for recursive implementation due to the recursion stack.

Example of Binary Search:

python

```python
def binary_search(arr, target):
    low, high = 0, len(arr) - 1
    while low <= high:
        mid = (low + high) // 2
        if arr[mid] == target:
```

```
        return mid  # Target found
    elif arr[mid] < target:
        low = mid + 1
    else:
        high = mid - 1
return -1  # Target not found


# Example usage
arr = [3, 9, 10, 27, 38, 43, 82]
result = binary_search(arr, 27)
print(result)  # Output: 3
```

Optimizing Merge Sort and Binary Search with Real-World Applications

1. Optimizing Merge Sort

While **Merge Sort** is already efficient with a time complexity of O(n log n), it can be optimized in several ways:

Iterative Merge Sort: Instead of using recursion, which has a space complexity of O(log n), you can use an **iterative merge sort** to reduce recursion stack overhead. This approach uses a bottom-up strategy, starting with smaller subarrays and merging them iteratively.

In-place Merge Sort: Traditional merge sort requires O(n) additional space for the temporary arrays. An **in-place merge sort** can be implemented to reduce the space complexity, but it can be more complex to code.

136

2. Optimizing Binary Search

In practice, **binary search** can be optimized further in certain scenarios:

For non-sorted data, you may first need to sort the data (which would be O(n log n) for most algorithms). However, once sorted, binary search gives you an efficient way to search in O(log n) time.

Using binary search with data structures: In **search trees** like AVL trees or Red-Black trees, binary search is used to find nodes. Since these trees are balanced, the search operations can be done efficiently in O(log n) time.

Practical Tips for Using Divide and Conquer in Competitive Programming

In competitive programming, efficiency is crucial, and divide and conquer strategies are frequently used. Here are some practical tips for applying divide and conquer in such contests:

Understand the Problem Constraints: Divide and conquer algorithms, like merge sort and quicksort, perform best when you know the input data is large and the problem can be broken down into smaller subproblems. Always analyze the constraints to determine if divide and conquer is the best approach.

Choosing the Right Sorting Algorithm:

> Use **merge sort** when you need stable sorting or when the dataset is very large and you can't afford the worst-case time complexity of quicksort.

> Use **quicksort** when performance is key and you expect the data to be "random" or well-distributed, ensuring a good pivot selection.

Binary Search for Optimization: In many search problems, binary search is the optimal choice. Whether you're searching for a target in a sorted array or deciding the feasibility of a solution (e.g., in **binary search on answer** problems), binary search can often reduce the time complexity from $O(n)$ to $O(\log n)$.

Preprocessing for Binary Search: Sometimes, binary search can be applied more efficiently if the array or dataset is preprocessed. For example, if you are asked to find a threshold in an array, sorting the array first allows you to apply binary search in logarithmic time.

Iterative Solutions: Whenever possible, try to use iterative solutions to avoid deep recursion, especially in a language like Python where recursion depth can be limited. For example, implement an **iterative merge sort** or **iterative binary search** to reduce space complexity.

Divide and Conquer for Graph Problems: In problems that involve **finding connected components** or **shortest paths**, divide and conquer can help break down the problem efficiently, especially when combined with algorithms like **Dijkstra's** or **Kruskal's** for graph-based challenges.

Use of Heaps in Divide and Conquer: For certain problems (e.g., finding the kth largest element in an array), using a **heap** can make divide and conquer more efficient by allowing you to build subproblems and maintain the results in logarithmic time.

Conclusion

In this chapter, we explored **divide and conquer** as a powerful algorithm design strategy, particularly for **sorting** and **searching**. We analyzed how divide and conquer is applied in **merge sort** and **quicksort**, two of the most commonly used sorting algorithms, and discussed optimizations for both. We also examined how **binary search** works within this paradigm, and how it can be leveraged for efficient searching in sorted arrays or search trees.

Finally, we provided **practical tips for competitive programming**, emphasizing the importance of choosing the right algorithms based on problem constraints and data characteristics. Divide and conquer remains one of the most effective strategies for solving large-scale problems in computer science and programming contests.

CHAPTER 13

TIME AND SPACE TRADE-OFFS: FINDING THE BEST BALANCE

In algorithm design, achieving optimal performance often requires making trade-offs between **time complexity** and **space complexity**. While you can optimize for one aspect, it may come at the cost of the other. Understanding and balancing these two factors is crucial for creating efficient algorithms, particularly when working with large datasets or real-time systems.

In this chapter, we will explore:

Trade-offs between time complexity and space complexity.

When it's worth sacrificing space for speed.

An example of trade-offs between quicksort and mergesort.

How to measure the effect of optimization decisions.

Understanding Trade-offs Between Time Complexity and Space Complexity

Time complexity and **space complexity** are two fundamental metrics used to evaluate the efficiency of an algorithm:

Time complexity measures the amount of time an algorithm takes to complete as a function of the input size.

Space complexity measures the amount of memory or storage an algorithm needs as a function of the input size.

While these two factors are related, optimizing for one can often lead to an increase in the other:

Optimizing for Time: An algorithm that runs faster might use more memory. For instance, caching intermediate results or precomputing values may speed up an algorithm at the cost of using extra memory.

Optimizing for Space: An algorithm that uses less memory may need to take more time to complete. For example, using an iterative approach instead of recursion can save memory but may increase the number of operations.

These trade-offs are essential when designing algorithms for systems with limited resources or when you need to balance performance with available memory.

When Is It Worth Sacrificing Space for Speed?

In certain cases, it is worth **sacrificing space for speed**. This happens when the performance requirements are more critical than the memory constraints. Here are a few scenarios where this trade-off makes sense:

Real-Time Systems: In real-time systems, where speed is crucial, algorithms that optimize for **faster execution** (time complexity) may be preferred, even if they use more memory.

Large-Scale Data Processing: When dealing with very large datasets, you might opt to use **extra memory** to store intermediate results to speed up computations, especially when waiting for results could be time-prohibitive.

When CPU Time is More Expensive than Memory: If you're working in a system where processing power is limited (e.g., in mobile devices or low-end hardware), but the available memory is abundant, it may make sense to use additional memory to avoid delays due to inefficient algorithms.

Caching and Memoization: For problems that involve overlapping subproblems (e.g., dynamic programming), caching intermediate results in memory (which uses

143

space) can reduce the time complexity, significantly improving the performance of the algorithm.

Example: Consider **memoization** in dynamic programming. Memoization involves storing the results of function calls to avoid recomputing them, which consumes additional space. However, this space usage dramatically reduces the overall time complexity of problems like the **Fibonacci sequence**, which would otherwise have an exponential time complexity if computed recursively.

Practical Example: Memoization for Fibonacci Numbers

Without memoization, the recursive Fibonacci algorithm has an exponential time complexity of $O(2^n)$. Using memoization, we can store the intermediate results and reduce the time complexity to $O(n)$.

python

```python
def fibonacci(n, memo={}):
    if n in memo:
        return memo[n]
    if n <= 1:
        return n
    memo[n] = fibonacci(n - 1, memo) + fibonacci(n - 2, memo)
    return memo[n]

# Example usage
```

```
print(fibonacci(10))   # Output: 55
```

This approach sacrifices space (due to the `memo` dictionary), but it dramatically speeds up the calculation.

Example: Trade-offs Between Quicksort and Mergesort

Let's examine how **quicksort** and **mergesort** illustrate the trade-offs between time and space complexities:

Quick Sort:

Time Complexity:

Best and Average Case: O(n log n)

Worst Case: O(n²) (when the pivot selection is poor)

Space Complexity: O(log n) (for the recursion stack)

Advantages:

Faster in practice for most cases due to lower constant factors.

In-place sorting (does not require additional space for arrays).

Disadvantages:

Worst-case time complexity can degrade to $O(n^2)$ if a poor pivot is selected.

Recursive calls can lead to stack overflow in the case of deep recursion (for large datasets).

Merge Sort:

Time Complexity: $O(n \log n)$ in all cases.

Space Complexity: $O(n)$ (due to the extra space used for the left and right halves during the merge step)

Advantages:

Predictable time complexity (always $O(n \log n)$).

Stable sorting (preserves the relative order of equal elements).

Disadvantages:

Requires extra space for temporary arrays, making it less memory-efficient than quicksort.

Slower than quicksort in practice for smaller arrays, due to additional memory usage and overhead.

When to Use Quicksort vs Merge Sort:

Quick Sort is preferred when you need an in-place, fast algorithm for general-purpose sorting. However, you must be careful of its worst-case behavior, especially for nearly sorted data.

Merge Sort is preferred when you need **stable sorting** and guaranteed **O(n log n)** time complexity, or when the array is too large to fit into memory (as merge sort can be implemented as an external sorting algorithm).

How to Measure the Effect of Optimization Decisions

When making optimization decisions, especially concerning the trade-offs between time and space, it is crucial to **measure the impact** of your decisions to understand the benefits and drawbacks. Here are a few strategies to measure the effect of optimization:

1. Benchmarking:

Benchmarking involves measuring the performance of your algorithm in terms of **execution time** and **memory usage**. This can be done by running your algorithm with different inputs and comparing the results.

Time Benchmarking: Use the `time` **module** in Python or other timing tools to measure the time it takes for an algorithm to run on different input sizes.

147

Example of Time Benchmarking:

```python
python

import time

start_time = time.time()
fibonacci(35)  # Example function call
end_time = time.time()

print(f"Execution time: {end_time - start_time} seconds")
```

Memory Benchmarking: Use memory profiling tools like **memory_profiler** in Python to measure the memory usage of your algorithm.

Example of Memory Benchmarking:

```python
python

from memory_profiler import profile

@profile
def example_function():
    arr = [i for i in range(1000000)]
    return arr

example_function()
```

2. Big-O Analysis:

When optimizing algorithms, it's essential to analyze the **theoretical time and space complexity** using **Big-O notation**. Comparing the complexities of different algorithms can help you make decisions about which trade-offs are most appropriate for your situation.

3. Stress Testing:

Test your algorithms with **large datasets** to see how they perform under extreme conditions. Stress testing allows you to evaluate whether an algorithm can handle real-world use cases and whether its performance meets the required thresholds.

4. Memory Profiling:

Use **profiling tools** to track memory usage throughout the execution of your algorithm. This can help you identify memory hotspots and decide where to reduce memory usage or trade memory for speed.

5. Empirical Testing:

Sometimes, the theoretical analysis may not fully reflect the real-world performance due to factors like hardware, system load, and input characteristics. In such cases, **empirical testing**—running your algorithm under real conditions and collecting data on time and space usage—can help you make a more informed decision.

Conclusion

In this chapter, we explored the trade-offs between **time complexity** and **space complexity** in algorithm design. We discussed when it is worthwhile to sacrifice space for speed, particularly in real-time systems or large-scale data processing. By analyzing **quicksort** and **mergesort**, we saw how space efficiency and time efficiency can influence the choice of algorithm depending on the problem at hand.

We also highlighted how to measure the impact of optimization decisions using **benchmarking**, **Big-O analysis**, **stress testing**, and **memory profiling**. Understanding and balancing these trade-offs is essential for creating algorithms that are not only efficient but also scalable and practical for real-world applications.

By carefully considering time and space trade-offs and measuring the effects of your optimization decisions, you can build more efficient algorithms suited to specific use cases and constraints.

CHAPTER 14

ADVANCED SEARCHING TECHNIQUES: HASHING AND BINARY SEARCH TREES

Efficient searching is a cornerstone of computer science and software development. Searching algorithms are crucial for tasks ranging from **data retrieval** to **optimization** and **query processing**. In this chapter, we will explore **advanced searching techniques**, focusing on **hash tables, binary search trees (BSTs)**, and **balanced trees**. These data structures provide highly optimized methods for storing and retrieving data, and understanding how to use them is essential for building high-performance systems.

This chapter will cover:

Optimizing search with hash tables and hash maps.

How binary search trees and AVL trees improve search efficiency.

Real-world applications: Implementing efficient data retrieval systems.

The role of balanced trees in reducing search time.

Optimizing Search with Hash Tables and Hash Maps

Hashing is one of the most powerful techniques for optimizing search operations. Hash tables and hash maps offer constant time complexity (O(1)) for search, insert, and delete operations on average, making them extremely efficient for scenarios where fast lookups are required.

1. Hash Tables and Hash Maps

A **hash table** (or **hash map**) is a data structure that stores key-value pairs. It uses a **hash function** to compute an index (also called a hash code) from the key, and this index is used to store the corresponding value in an array. The key-value pair is then stored at the computed index in the table.

Time Complexity:

Average Case: O(1) for search, insert, and delete.

Worst Case: O(n) in case of hash collisions (when multiple keys map to the same index).

Space Complexity: O(n), where n is the number of elements stored in the hash table.

2. How Hashing Works

Hash Function: A function that takes an input (key) and returns a fixed-size integer (hash value). This hash value is used as the index in the array where the value is stored.

Handling Collisions: When two keys map to the same index (collision), several techniques can be used to handle this:

Chaining: Store multiple elements at the same index using a list or linked list.

Open Addressing: If a collision occurs, try to find another open slot in the table (e.g., linear probing, quadratic probing).

3. Example of Hash Table with Chaining:

python

```python
class HashTable:
    def __init__(self, size):
        self.size = size
        self.table = [[] for _ in range(self.size)]  # List of empty lists for chaining

    def _hash(self, key):
        return hash(key) % self.size  # Simple hash function
```

```
    def insert(self, key, value):
        index = self._hash(key)
        for kv in self.table[index]:
            if kv[0] == key:  # If the key exists,
update its value
                kv[1] = value
                return
        self.table[index].append([key,    value])
# Add the key-value pair

    def search(self, key):
        index = self._hash(key)
        for kv in self.table[index]:
            if kv[0] == key:
                return kv[1]  # Return the value
associated with the key
        return None  # Key not found

# Example usage
ht = HashTable(10)
ht.insert("apple", 10)
ht.insert("banana", 20)
print(ht.search("apple"))   # Output: 10
print(ht.search("orange"))  # Output: None
```

In this example, the hash table stores key-value pairs using **chaining** to handle collisions. The insert function checks for existing keys and appends the new key-value pair to the list at the computed index.

4. Applications of Hash Tables

Caching: Hash maps are widely used for caching in applications, where results of expensive function calls are stored for quick retrieval.

Databases: Hash tables are used for indexing in databases, speeding up data retrieval operations.

Symbol Tables: In compilers, hash tables are used to store variables and function names.

How Binary Search Trees and AVL Trees Improve Search Efficiency

Binary Search Trees (BSTs) and **AVL trees** are data structures that allow for fast searching by maintaining sorted order. **BSTs** ensure that for any given node:

The left subtree contains only nodes with values less than the node's value.

The right subtree contains only nodes with values greater than the node's value.

This property allows for efficient searching, insertion, and deletion operations. However, in an unbalanced BST, the time

155

complexity can degrade to O(n), making it inefficient. To overcome this, **AVL trees** and other **self-balancing trees** maintain balance during operations.

1. Binary Search Trees (BSTs)

A **binary search tree (BST)** allows for efficient searching, inserting, and deleting of elements, assuming the tree is balanced.

Time Complexity:

> Best Case (Balanced BST): O(log n) for search, insert, and delete.

> Worst Case (Unbalanced BST): O(n), when the tree becomes a linked list (e.g., when the elements are inserted in sorted order).

Example of a Simple Binary Search Tree:

python

```python
class Node:
    def __init__(self, value):
        self.value = value
        self.left = None
        self.right = None

class BST:
```

```python
def __init__(self):
    self.root = None

def insert(self, value):
    if self.root is None:
        self.root = Node(value)
    else:
        self._insert(self.root, value)

def _insert(self, node, value):
    if value < node.value:
        if node.left is None:
            node.left = Node(value)
        else:
            self._insert(node.left, value)
    elif value > node.value:
        if node.right is None:
            node.right = Node(value)
        else:
            self._insert(node.right, value)

def search(self, value):
    return self._search(self.root, value)

def _search(self, node, value):
    if node is None or node.value == value:
        return node
    if value < node.value:
```

```
            return           self._search(node.left,
value)
        return self._search(node.right, value)

# Example usage
bst = BST()
bst.insert(10)
bst.insert(20)
bst.insert(5)
node = bst.search(20)
print(node.value if node else "Not found")    #
Output: 20
```

2. AVL Trees (Self-Balancing BSTs)

An **AVL tree** is a self-balancing binary search tree that automatically maintains its balance during insertions and deletions. The height difference between the left and right subtrees of any node is at most 1. If an insertion or deletion causes this balance to be violated, the tree is **rebalanced** using rotations.

Time Complexity:

O(log n) for search, insert, and delete (since the tree remains balanced).

Space Complexity: O(n) for storing the nodes.

158

Example of Rotations in AVL Trees:

Left Rotation: Used when the right subtree is too heavy.

Right Rotation: Used when the left subtree is too heavy.

Double Rotations: A combination of left and right rotations for balancing.

Real-World Applications: Implementing Efficient Data Retrieval Systems

Efficient searching is critical in many real-world systems. Here are some examples of where advanced search techniques, such as hash tables and balanced trees, are used:

1. Databases and Indexing:

Databases use **hash maps** for indexing large datasets, allowing for fast data retrieval. In addition, **B-trees** (a type of self-balancing tree) are used for indexing in databases, providing efficient range queries.

Real-World Example: When you query a database for a specific record (e.g., finding a user by their ID), the database might use a **hash table** for quick lookups, or **B-trees** for efficient range searches (e.g., finding all records within a certain date range).

159

2. File Systems:

Modern file systems use **hashing** and **binary search trees** for efficient file retrieval. For instance, **ext4** uses a **hash table** to manage inodes, and **B-trees** for directory indexing.

> **Real-World Example**: When you search for a file on your computer, the file system may use a **hash table** to quickly find the file's inode or metadata, allowing for faster access to file contents.

3. Memory Management:

In **memory allocation systems**, efficient search techniques like hash tables or balanced trees are used to allocate, free, and manage blocks of memory.

> **Real-World Example**: When allocating memory dynamically in a system, **hash tables** can be used to manage memory blocks, while **AVL trees** or **B-trees** may be used to manage free memory blocks and ensure fast allocation.

The Role of Balanced Trees in Reducing Search Time

Balanced trees, such as **AVL trees** and **Red-Black trees**, play a critical role in improving the efficiency of search operations by ensuring that the tree remains balanced. In an unbalanced tree, the

160

time complexity for searching can degrade to O(n), which can be unacceptable for large datasets.

By maintaining balance, these trees ensure that the **height** of the tree is always logarithmic in terms of the number of nodes, guaranteeing that search operations are efficient (O(log n)) even in the worst case.

> **Real-World Example**: In databases, balanced trees like **B-trees** and **B+ trees** are used for indexing, ensuring that even large datasets can be searched efficiently. These trees are optimized for systems that read and write large blocks of data, such as **disk-based databases**.

Conclusion

In this chapter, we explored advanced searching techniques, including **hashing** with hash tables and hash maps, as well as **binary search trees (BSTs)** and **AVL trees**. We saw how these data structures improve search efficiency by offering faster lookups, even for large datasets. We also discussed the role of balanced trees in maintaining efficient search times, reducing the search time complexity from O(n) to O(log n).

Finally, we highlighted real-world applications where these techniques are used, including in **databases**, **file systems**, and **memory management**. Understanding these advanced search algorithms and data structures is crucial for designing efficient systems and algorithms in a wide range of applications.

CHAPTER 15

MEMORY MANAGEMENT AND ALGORITHM OPTIMIZATION

In algorithm design, **memory management** plays a critical role in optimizing performance, particularly when working with large datasets or memory-constrained environments. Efficient memory management can reduce the **space complexity** of an algorithm, improving its overall efficiency and allowing it to handle larger inputs without running into memory-related issues such as **out-of-memory errors** or performance degradation.

In this chapter, we will explore:

How memory management affects algorithm performance.

Techniques for managing memory in large datasets.

Optimizing space complexity with memory-efficient data structures.

Real-world examples of handling memory issues in applications.

How Memory Management Affects Algorithm Performance

Memory management significantly impacts the performance of algorithms in several ways:

Space Complexity: An algorithm's space complexity refers to the amount of memory it requires relative to the input size. Algorithms with higher space complexity consume more memory, which can lead to slower performance or memory exhaustion in environments with limited resources.

Garbage Collection: In languages like Python or Java, memory management is handled through **garbage collection**. However, inefficient memory usage can cause excessive garbage collection, leading to **performance overhead**. For instance, frequent allocation and deallocation of memory can lead to fragmentation, where free memory is scattered across the system.

Cache Locality: The way memory is accessed affects the **cache locality** of an algorithm. Accessing data in contiguous memory locations improves cache performance, reducing the latency involved in fetching data from RAM.

Memory Allocation and Deallocation: Inefficient memory allocation and deallocation can create issues like memory leaks (where memory is not properly released) or excessive allocation, both of which can degrade algorithm performance. Memory management must be done carefully to avoid these pitfalls.

External Storage: When working with **large datasets** that cannot fit in main memory (RAM), algorithms may need to use **external storage** (e.g., disk-based databases or distributed storage systems). Managing data transfer between memory and disk can have a significant impact on the overall performance of the algorithm.

Techniques for Managing Memory in Large Datasets

When dealing with **large datasets**, memory management becomes crucial. Here are several techniques for optimizing memory usage when handling large datasets:

1. Streaming and Lazy Evaluation

Instead of loading the entire dataset into memory, **streaming** or **lazy evaluation** techniques process the data in chunks or streams. This reduces memory usage by only holding a small portion of the data in memory at any given time.

Lazy Evaluation: In languages like Python, lazy evaluation allows for processing elements only when they are needed, such as when working with **generators** or

iterators. This reduces memory usage because intermediate results are not stored in memory.

Example: A Python generator for lazy evaluation:

python

```
def generate_numbers(n):
    for i in range(n):
        yield i  # Lazily yields one number
at a time

# Using the generator to process large data
without loading it all at once
for num in generate_numbers(1000000):
    print(num)
```

2. In-place Algorithms

In-place algorithms modify the input data directly, reducing the need for extra space. These algorithms use a constant amount of space ($O(1)$) in contrast to algorithms that create copies of the data.

Example: **In-place sorting algorithms**, like **quicksort**, modify the input array without requiring additional memory, as opposed to algorithms like **merge sort** that need extra space for temporary arrays.

166

3. Efficient Data Structures

Choosing the right data structure is crucial for managing memory efficiently. Some data structures are more memory-efficient than others, and choosing the right one can lead to significant reductions in space complexity.

Arrays vs. Linked Lists: Arrays are more memory-efficient for storing elements contiguously, but linked lists can be more flexible when the number of elements changes frequently.

Dynamic Arrays: If you need a dynamic array (e.g., lists in Python), ensure that it resizes efficiently. Avoid using data structures that over-allocate memory when not necessary.

Memory-Efficient Trees: For large hierarchical data, using **balanced binary search trees (BSTs)** or **B-trees** reduces memory overhead by keeping the tree's height logarithmic relative to the number of nodes.

4. Compression Techniques

When working with large datasets that consist of repetitive or predictable data, using **compression algorithms** (e.g., **gzip**, **LZ77**) can reduce memory usage by storing data in a compressed

167

form. Compression can be particularly useful when dealing with text, images, or other media types.

Lossless Compression: Compress data without losing any information (e.g., **Huffman coding**).

Lossy Compression: For non-critical data, lossy compression (e.g., **JPEG** for images) can be used to drastically reduce memory usage by sacrificing some level of fidelity.

5. Memory Pooling

Memory pooling is a technique where memory is pre-allocated and reused from a pool of memory blocks, reducing the need for dynamic allocation and deallocation, which can be costly in terms of time and space. Memory pooling is commonly used in systems that require high-performance memory management, such as game development or real-time systems.

Optimizing Space Complexity with Memory-Efficient Data Structures

To optimize space complexity, it's essential to choose memory-efficient data structures that use the least amount of memory while still providing the necessary functionality. Here are some memory-efficient data structures:

1. Hash Tables

While hash tables provide O(1) time complexity for search, insertion, and deletion, they can be memory-heavy, especially when dealing with large datasets. Optimizing a hash table involves:

Choosing an appropriate size for the table to minimize the **load factor**.

Using open addressing or **chaining** to manage collisions efficiently.

2. Trie (Prefix Tree)

A **trie** is a tree-like data structure that efficiently stores strings or sequences. It uses shared prefixes to minimize space usage compared to storing each string independently. Tries are particularly useful in applications like **autocomplete** and **spell-checking**.

3. Bloom Filters

A **Bloom filter** is a probabilistic data structure that allows for space-efficient membership testing. It uses multiple hash functions to map elements to a bit array. Bloom filters are useful when you need to test for the existence of an element without storing the entire set, but they come with a risk of false positives.

4. Bit Arrays

A **bit array** (or **bit vector**) is a memory-efficient structure that uses a single bit to represent each element. They are particularly useful when you need to store boolean values, such as in **set operations** or **sparse data representations**.

5. Sparse Matrices

For datasets that are primarily zeros or empty values (e.g., large matrices with few non-zero entries), **sparse matrices** are more memory-efficient. They store only non-zero elements and their positions, reducing space complexity.

Example: Handling Memory Issues in Real-World Applications

Let's consider a real-world application where **memory management** is critical: a **web server** handling large numbers of concurrent requests. In such systems, efficiently managing memory can have a significant impact on performance and scalability.

Scenario: Memory Management in a Web Server

A web server processes requests and serves data to users. The server needs to manage incoming data efficiently, especially when handling large datasets (e.g., video streaming or large file uploads). If the server stores each file or request in memory, it could quickly run out of resources.

Solution:

Streaming Data: Rather than loading entire files into memory, the server can use **streaming** techniques to process data in chunks, reducing memory usage.

Compression: The server can compress large files before storing them in memory or sending them over the network, thereby reducing the amount of memory used for storing the data.

Caching: The server can use a **cache** (e.g., in-memory cache using a hash table) to store frequently accessed data, allowing for quick retrieval without recalculating or fetching data from disk.

Memory Pooling: The server can use **memory pooling** to allocate memory for request processing, reducing the overhead of dynamic memory allocation and improving the server's responsiveness.

By applying memory management techniques such as **streaming**, **compression**, and **caching**, the web server can handle large numbers of concurrent requests without running into memory bottlenecks or performance degradation.

Conclusion

In this chapter, we explored the critical role of **memory management** in optimizing algorithm performance, particularly when dealing with **large datasets**. We covered several techniques for managing memory efficiently, such as **streaming**, **lazy evaluation**, **in-place algorithms**, and **compression**. We also discussed the use of **memory-efficient data structures** like **hash tables**, **tries**, and **Bloom filters** to optimize space complexity.

Real-world applications, particularly in web servers and large-scale systems, can greatly benefit from these techniques by improving memory usage and ensuring that systems can scale efficiently. Understanding how to manage memory effectively allows developers to build high-performance applications that can handle large datasets without running into memory-related issues.

CHAPTER 16

OPTIMIZING NESTED LOOPS AND MULTI-LEVEL ALGORITHMS

In many algorithmic problems, **nested loops** are used to process multi-dimensional data or perform operations that involve multiple levels of iteration. However, nested loops often lead to higher time complexities, especially when the loops are deeply nested. Optimizing these loops is crucial for improving algorithm performance, particularly when working with large datasets.

In this chapter, we will cover:

Strategies to reduce the complexity of nested loops.

How to optimize multi-level loops for performance.

Example: Matrix multiplication and optimizations.

Identifying and eliminating inefficient nested iterations.

Strategies to Reduce the Complexity of Nested Loops

Nested loops are typically used to process two or more collections of data. If not optimized, nested loops can lead to high time complexity, especially when the inner loop's execution depends on the outer loop.

1. Reducing the Problem Size

The first strategy for optimizing nested loops is to **reduce the size of the problem** being processed. This can often be done by:

- **Dividing the problem** into smaller subproblems (using techniques like **divide and conquer** or **dynamic programming**).

- **Eliminating unnecessary iterations**: Sometimes, not all iterations are needed. By keeping track of results or using auxiliary data structures, you can avoid recalculating values multiple times.

2. Breaking Early (Early Termination)

In some problems, it is possible to break out of the loop early if certain conditions are met. This can help eliminate unnecessary iterations, reducing the overall complexity.

Break or return early if a solution has been found or if further iterations would not provide useful results.

3. Using Efficient Data Structures

Choosing the right data structure can sometimes eliminate the need for nested iterations:

Hash tables can help you avoid redundant lookups by storing and retrieving data in constant time ($O(1)$).

Binary Search Trees (BSTs) or **Heaps** can improve searching operations, reducing the need for nested iterations in some problems.

4. Optimizing the Inner Loop

Often, the performance bottleneck is the **inner loop**. To optimize the inner loop, you can:

Use memoization or caching to store intermediate results, preventing the need to recompute the same values.

Preprocess the data: Sorting or rearranging data before starting the loops can often eliminate unnecessary comparisons or calculations within the inner loop.

5. Parallelization

For certain types of problems, the work done in the inner and outer loops can be parallelized. By splitting the work among multiple threads or processors, you can significantly reduce execution time.

Multi-threading or **distributed computing** frameworks like **MapReduce** can be used to run multiple iterations concurrently.

How to Optimize Multi-level Loops for Performance

When dealing with multi-level loops, where each loop is nested within another, the complexity grows quickly. In such cases, it's essential to optimize the loops in the following ways:

1. Refactor the Algorithm

Try to **refactor** the algorithm so that the need for multiple nested loops is reduced:

Sometimes, nested loops can be transformed into a **single loop** by reorganizing the problem into a different form (e.g., using a single data structure that holds multiple related values).

For example, if you're working with a **2D array** and iterating through each row and column, you may consider flattening the 2D array into a 1D array, which would remove the need for nested loops.

2. Using Dynamic Programming

For problems with overlapping subproblems, **dynamic programming (DP)** can often replace the need for multiple nested iterations. By storing results of subproblems, you can avoid recalculating the same solutions and reduce the time complexity.

For example, **Fibonacci** calculations with recursion lead to a lot of repeated work. By using DP (either through memoization or tabulation), you can reduce the time complexity from $O(2^n)$ to $O(n)$.

3. Loop Unrolling

Loop unrolling is an optimization technique where you manually expand the loop to perform multiple iterations within one pass of the loop. This can reduce the overhead of repeated checks and improve performance, especially in low-level programming or performance-critical applications.

Example: Matrix Multiplication and Optimizations

Matrix multiplication is a common operation in many scientific and engineering applications, but it often involves nested loops, leading to high time complexity.

177

1. Naive Matrix Multiplication

The naive matrix multiplication algorithm involves three nested loops to multiply two matrices AAA and BBB to get matrix CCC. If matrix AAA is of size m×nm \times nm×n and matrix BBB is of size n×pn \times pn×p, the resulting matrix CCC will have dimensions m×pm \times pm×p. The time complexity of this naive approach is O(m×n×p)O(m \times n \times p)O(m×n×p).

Example of Naive Matrix Multiplication:

python

```
def matrix_multiply(A, B):
    m, n = len(A), len(B)
    p = len(B[0])
    C = [[0] * p for _ in range(m)]

    for i in range(m):
        for j in range(p):
            for k in range(n):
                C[i][j] += A[i][k] * B[k][j]
    return C

# Example usage:
A = [[1, 2], [3, 4]]
B = [[5, 6], [7, 8]]
result = matrix_multiply(A, B)
print(result)  # Output: [[19, 22], [43, 50]]
```

Time Complexity: O(m × n × p)

Space Complexity: O(m × p) for the resulting matrix.

2. Optimizations for Matrix Multiplication

Matrix multiplication can be optimized in several ways:

- **Strassen's Algorithm**: Reduces the time complexity of matrix multiplication from $O(n3)O(n^3)O(n3)$ to approximately $O(n2.81)O(n^{2.81})O(n2.81)$. It uses a divide-and-conquer approach to recursively break down the matrix multiplication process.

- **Block Matrix Multiplication**: Instead of performing element-wise multiplication, divide the matrices into blocks and perform matrix multiplication on smaller submatrices (also known as **tiling**). This can improve cache performance and reduce memory access times.

For example, **Strassen's algorithm** involves breaking down the matrix multiplication problem into smaller subproblems and recursively solving them, thus reducing the number of operations.

3. Cache Optimization and Blocking

For large matrices, improving the way data is accessed can significantly speed up the multiplication process. A **cache-**

179

efficient algorithm for matrix multiplication divides the matrices into blocks, ensuring that the blocks fit into the CPU cache, reducing memory access time.

Example of Block Matrix Multiplication:

```python
python

def block_multiply(A, B, block_size):
    m, n = len(A), len(B)
    p = len(B[0])
    C = [[0] * p for _ in range(m)]

    for i in range(0, m, block_size):
        for j in range(0, p, block_size):
            for k in range(0, n, block_size):
                for x in range(i, min(i + block_size, m)):
                    for y in range(j, min(j + block_size, p)):
                        for z in range(k, min(k + block_size, n)):
                            C[x][y] += A[x][z] * B[z][y]
    return C

# Example usage with block size 2:
A = [[1, 2], [3, 4]]
B = [[5, 6], [7, 8]]
```

```
result = block_multiply(A, B, 2)
print(result)  # Output: [[19, 22], [43, 50]]
```

This approach improves cache locality and can significantly speed up matrix multiplication for large matrices.

Identifying and Eliminating Inefficient Nested Iterations

When working with nested iterations, there are several common inefficiencies to look for:

Unnecessary Repetitions: Make sure that the inner loop does not repeat computations that have already been done. For example, in a **sorting** algorithm, if you are comparing elements that have already been sorted, there's no need to revisit them.

Excessive Nested Loops: Sometimes, nested loops can be refactored into a more efficient algorithm. For example, if a problem involves finding the shortest path in a graph, an algorithm like **Dijkstra's** can be used to replace brute-force nested iterations.

Redundant Data Access: Avoid accessing the same data multiple times in nested loops. For example, instead of performing a search in each iteration of the inner loop, you could store the result in a variable or use a **hash table** for fast lookups.

Conclusion

In this chapter, we explored **strategies to optimize nested loops** and multi-level algorithms, which are essential for improving algorithm performance, especially when working with large datasets. We discussed techniques like **early termination**, **using efficient data structures**, and **reducing the problem size** to optimize nested iterations.

We also examined **matrix multiplication** and its optimizations, including **Strassen's algorithm** and **block matrix multiplication**, which can significantly reduce the time complexity of the operation.

By identifying inefficient nested iterations and leveraging these optimization techniques, you can improve the efficiency of your algorithms and ensure that they perform well even with large or complex datasets.

CHAPTER 17

UNDERSTANDING AND OPTIMIZING RECURSIVE ALGORITHMS

Recursion is a powerful tool in algorithm design, allowing you to break down complex problems into simpler, smaller subproblems. However, recursive algorithms can become inefficient due to issues like excessive recursion depth, repeated function calls, and stack overflow. Understanding and optimizing recursion is key to improving the performance of recursive algorithms, especially in large-scale problems or environments with limited resources.

In this chapter, we will cover:

Recursion depth and optimization techniques.

Reducing the overhead of recursion calls.

Examples: Optimizing recursive tree traversal and backtracking algorithms.

Recursion Depth and Optimization Techniques

Recursive algorithms work by repeatedly calling themselves with modified parameters until a **base case** is met. While recursion is elegant and intuitive for many problems, it can lead to high **recursion depth**, resulting in inefficiency and potential **stack overflow** errors.

1. Understanding Recursion Depth

Recursion depth refers to how many times a function calls itself before reaching the base case. The **depth** is a critical factor in determining both **space complexity** (due to the recursion stack) and **time complexity** (due to the number of recursive calls).

For example, in a **binary tree traversal**, the recursion depth corresponds to the height of the tree. A deep recursion tree with many levels may quickly use up the system's stack space, leading to **stack overflow** errors in languages like Python and Java (which limit recursion depth).

2. Tail Recursion Optimization

Tail recursion occurs when the recursive call is the last operation in the function. This is a key optimization because tail-recursive functions can be optimized by the compiler or interpreter into an **iterative loop**, removing the need to maintain multiple function calls in the recursion stack.

184

Time Complexity: O(n), just like the non-tail recursive version.

Space Complexity: O(1) after tail recursion optimization, as no additional stack frames are required.

In some languages (e.g., **Scheme, Haskell, Python 3**), tail recursion optimization (TRO) is supported, allowing recursive calls to be converted to loops, thereby reducing the risk of stack overflow.

Example of Tail Recursion:

python

```python
def factorial_tail(n, accumulator=1):
    if n == 0:
        return accumulator
    return factorial_tail(n - 1, n * accumulator)

# Example usage
print(factorial_tail(5))   # Output: 120
```

In this example, the recursive call is the last operation, and no further computation is needed after it returns, which makes the recursion tail-recursive.

3. Memoization

Memoization is a technique where you store the results of expensive function calls to avoid recomputing them. It is particularly useful for recursive algorithms that solve the same subproblems multiple times (e.g., Fibonacci, dynamic programming).

Memoization reduces both **time complexity** and **space complexity** by caching results and thus preventing redundant recursive calls.

> **Time Complexity**: O(n) for problems like Fibonacci or dynamic programming problems after memoization.

> **Space Complexity**: O(n) due to storing intermediate results.

Example of Memoization:

python

```python
def fibonacci(n, memo={}):
    if n in memo:
        return memo[n]
    if n <= 1:
        return n
    memo[n] = fibonacci(n - 1, memo) + fibonacci(n - 2, memo)
    return memo[n]
```

```
# Example usage
print(fibonacci(10))   # Output: 55
```

By storing already computed Fibonacci numbers in a dictionary, memoization ensures that each Fibonacci number is computed only once, significantly improving the performance compared to a naive recursive implementation.

Reducing the Overhead of Recursion Calls

One of the primary drawbacks of recursion is the **overhead** introduced by repeated function calls. Every recursive call adds a new **stack frame**, consuming both time (due to function call overhead) and memory (due to stack space). Here are a few strategies to reduce this overhead:

1. Using Iteration Instead of Recursion

When possible, converting recursive algorithms to **iterative solutions** can reduce the function call overhead and avoid stack overflow. This is particularly useful in problems where the recursive calls do not require a complex state to be saved between calls.

For example, an **in-order traversal** of a binary tree can be implemented iteratively using a stack, removing the need for deep recursion.

Example of Iterative In-order Traversal:

python

```python
def iterative_inorder_traversal(root):
    stack = []
    current = root
    while current or stack:
        while current:
            stack.append(current)
            current = current.left
        current = stack.pop()
        print(current.value, end=" ")
        current = current.right
```

In this example, the recursive in-order traversal is replaced with an iterative solution using a stack, eliminating the recursion depth problem.

2. Tail Call Optimization (TCO)

In languages that support **tail call optimization**, a recursive call that is the final action of a function can be optimized into an iterative loop, reducing the overhead of maintaining additional stack frames. This technique is especially useful when recursion is necessary but avoiding excessive function calls is crucial.

3. Hybrid Approach

For some problems, you can use a **hybrid approach** where the algorithm switches between recursion and iteration depending on the problem size. For instance, a **depth-first search (DFS)** can be implemented recursively for small graphs but iteratively for larger ones to prevent stack overflow.

Examples: Optimizing Recursive Tree Traversal and Backtracking Algorithms

1. Optimizing Recursive Tree Traversal

Tree traversal problems, such as **pre-order**, **in-order**, and **post-order** traversal of binary trees, are commonly solved with recursion. However, deep trees can lead to **stack overflow** issues in languages with limited recursion depth.

To optimize recursive tree traversal:

Iterative methods (like **Morris Traversal**) can be used to reduce recursion depth by employing threading techniques (though these are not always intuitive or easy to implement).

Tail recursion can be used for some types of tree traversal if the tree is balanced and the recursive calls are at the last step.

Example: Tail Recursion in Tree Traversal:

python

```python
class TreeNode:
    def __init__(self, value):
        self.value = value
        self.left = None
        self.right = None


def tail_recursive_inorder(root, result=None):
    if result is None:
        result = []
    if root:
        tail_recursive_inorder(root.left,
result)
        result.append(root.value)
        tail_recursive_inorder(root.right,
result)
    return result

# Example usage
root = TreeNode(1)
root.left = TreeNode(2)
root.right = TreeNode(3)
print(tail_recursive_inorder(root))    # Output:
[2, 1, 3]
```

2. Backtracking Algorithms

Backtracking is a technique used to solve problems that require exploring all possible solutions by trying different options, one at a time. For example, backtracking is commonly used in problems like:

Solving **Sudoku**.

Finding all subsets in a set.

N-Queens problem.

The challenge with backtracking algorithms is that they can have **deep recursion** due to the exploration of multiple branches of a solution space, making them prone to **stack overflow** or performance issues.

To optimize **backtracking**:

- **Prune the search space**: By using techniques like **branch pruning**, you can eliminate parts of the search space that do not lead to a valid solution, reducing the number of recursive calls.

- **Iterative Backtracking**: When deep recursion is a concern, you can convert a recursive backtracking algorithm into an **iterative solution** using a stack or queue.

Memoization: If the backtracking algorithm revisits the same subproblems, storing results (memoization) can prevent redundant work.

Example: N-Queens Backtracking:

python

```python
def solve_n_queens(n):
    def is_safe(board, row, col):
        for i in range(row):
            if board[i] == col or abs(board[i] -
col) == row - i:
                return False
        return True

    def solve(board, row):
        if row == n:
            solutions.append(board[:])
            return
        for col in range(n):
            if is_safe(board, row, col):
                board[row] = col
                solve(board, row + 1)
                board[row] = -1  # Backtrack

    solutions = []
    solve([-1] * n, 0)
    return solutions
```

```
# Example usage
n = 4
result = solve_n_queens(n)
print(result)  # Output: [[1, 3, 0, 2], [2, 0, 3,
1]]
```

In this example, the **N-Queens problem** is solved using backtracking. Optimizing this algorithm involves **pruning invalid branches** early, reducing unnecessary recursive calls.

Conclusion

In this chapter, we explored how to **optimize recursive algorithms** to improve performance and avoid common pitfalls like excessive recursion depth and stack overflow. We discussed techniques such as **tail recursion, memoization**, and **iterative solutions** to reduce the overhead of recursion.

We also examined real-world examples, including **tree traversal** and **backtracking algorithms**, demonstrating how to optimize these recursive approaches for performance. By understanding and applying these optimization techniques, you can build more efficient recursive algorithms that perform well even for large datasets or complex problems.

CHAPTER 18

USING CACHING TO IMPROVE ALGORITHM EFFICIENCY

In the world of algorithm design, **caching** is an essential optimization technique that can significantly improve the performance of algorithms by storing intermediate results and reusing them, especially for problems that involve repeated computations. Whether you're working with dynamic programming, search algorithms, or sorting algorithms, caching can save time by avoiding redundant calculations, ultimately improving the overall efficiency of your programs.

In this chapter, we will cover:

Introduction to caching and its benefits.

How to apply caching in algorithms for repeated computations.

Example: Memoization in dynamic programming problems.

Cache strategies for optimizing search and sorting algorithms.

Introduction to Caching and Its Benefits

Caching is the process of storing the results of expensive function calls or computations in memory so that future requests for the same results can be retrieved quickly without recalculating them. The primary goal of caching is to reduce the **time complexity** of repetitive operations by making previously computed results easily accessible.

Key Benefits of Caching:

Improved Speed: By storing intermediate results, caching reduces the need for repeated calculations, leading to faster execution.

Memory Efficiency: Although caching consumes memory, it can drastically reduce the time complexity, making it a worthwhile trade-off in many cases.

Reduced Latency: Caching can help reduce the response time for retrieving data or results, particularly in real-time applications or web services.

Optimization in Dynamic Problems: Caching is particularly useful in **dynamic programming (DP)** problems where the same subproblems are solved multiple times.

Where Caching Is Useful:

Recursive Algorithms: In algorithms that involve recursion (e.g., Fibonacci sequence, tree traversals), caching intermediate results can avoid redundant calculations.

Database Queries: Caching is used in web applications to store frequently accessed data, reducing the number of database queries.

Web Content: Caching frequently accessed web pages or assets can reduce server load and improve user experience.

How to Apply Caching in Algorithms for Repeated Computations

One of the most common applications of caching in algorithms is **memoization**, which is a specific form of caching used in recursive algorithms. Memoization stores the results of function calls and reuses them when the same inputs occur again, avoiding redundant computation.

1. Memoization (Top-down Caching)

Memoization is a technique that involves caching results for function calls to avoid recalculating them. In a **top-down** approach, the algorithm computes the result recursively and stores the intermediate results in a cache (often a dictionary or hash map).

Time Complexity: O(n) for problems like Fibonacci, after memoization.

Space Complexity: O(n) for storing the intermediate results.

2. Tabulation (Bottom-up Caching)

Tabulation is another technique used in dynamic programming. Unlike memoization, tabulation builds the solution iteratively from the bottom up. It involves filling a table (usually an array) with results of smaller subproblems.

Time Complexity: O(n) (depending on the problem).

Space Complexity: O(n) for storing results.

Memoization is usually easier to implement since it requires fewer changes to the original recursive algorithm, but tabulation can sometimes be more efficient in terms of space usage and avoids recursion stack overhead.

Example: Memoization in Dynamic Programming Problems

One of the most common examples of caching is **memoization in dynamic programming (DP)**. Let's look at the **Fibonacci sequence** as an example. Without caching, the recursive approach to calculating Fibonacci numbers results in redundant calculations, leading to exponential time complexity.

Naive Recursive Fibonacci:

python

```python
def fibonacci(n):
    if n <= 1:
        return n
    return fibonacci(n - 1) + fibonacci(n - 2)

# Example usage
print(fibonacci(10))   # Output: 55
```

This naive approach has an **exponential time complexity** of $O(2^n)$, as it recomputes the same Fibonacci numbers multiple times.

Optimized Fibonacci Using Memoization:

By using **memoization**, we store the results of previously computed Fibonacci numbers, so they don't need to be recomputed. This reduces the time complexity to $O(n)$.

python

```python
def fibonacci_memo(n, memo={}):
    if n in memo:
        return memo[n]
```

```
if n <= 1:
    return n
memo[n] = fibonacci_memo(n - 1, memo) +
fibonacci_memo(n - 2, memo)
    return memo[n]


# Example usage
print(fibonacci_memo(10))   # Output: 55
```

Time Complexity: O(n) due to memoization.

Space Complexity: O(n) to store the intermediate results in the memo dictionary.

This optimized solution is much faster, especially for large n, and ensures that each Fibonacci number is computed only once.

Cache Strategies for Optimizing Search and Sorting Algorithms

1. Optimizing Binary Search with Caching

While **binary search** itself is a very efficient search algorithm with O(log n) time complexity, caching can be used to optimize cases where binary search is repeatedly applied to the same dataset or elements.

For example, when performing binary search over the same sorted array multiple times, caching the results of previous searches can save time.

Cache the Results: Store the result of each binary search operation in a cache so that you don't have to perform the binary search again for the same element.

2. Optimizing Sorting Algorithms with Caching

Although sorting algorithms like **quicksort** or **merge sort** do not directly benefit from caching in a traditional sense, there are **optimizations** that can be made with caching:

Avoid Re-Sorting: If the array is already partially sorted or if the same set of elements is being sorted multiple times, caching the results of partial sorts or sorted arrays can save time.

Memoization in Sorting: In certain algorithms, such as **radix sort** or **bucket sort**, caching intermediate results or previously computed values (like previously sorted buckets) can improve performance.

Real-World Examples of Caching

1. Web Caching

In web development, caching is commonly used to store frequently accessed web pages, database query results, or API responses to reduce server load and improve response times. Caching strategies such as **LRU (Least Recently Used), LFU**

(Least Frequently Used), or **TTL (Time to Live)** can be employed to control cache size and eviction policies.

> **Example**: A **web server** may cache the result of a complex database query (such as retrieving user information) so that the same query doesn't need to be repeated on every user request.

2. Database Query Caching

Databases use **query caching** to store the results of database queries and reuse them for future queries with the same parameters. This can significantly reduce the time it takes to retrieve data and avoid unnecessary processing.

> **Example**: **MySQL** or **Redis** can cache the result of SELECT queries, reducing the need to perform expensive database operations repeatedly.

3. Image Caching in Applications

In image-heavy applications (such as social media or image galleries), caching is used to store frequently accessed images either in **memory** (RAM) or on **disk**. By caching images, applications can avoid reloading or reprocessing images from disk or external sources.

Example: An image gallery app may cache thumbnail versions of images to speed up subsequent views of the same image.

4. Machine Learning Model Inference

When deploying machine learning models for inference, caching is used to store intermediate results of **model predictions** or **preprocessed data**. This can significantly speed up predictions, especially in real-time applications where the same inputs are queried multiple times.

Example: A **recommendation system** might cache the results of user recommendations or previously computed similarity metrics to avoid recalculating them for each new user request.

Conclusion

In this chapter, we explored how **caching** can dramatically improve algorithm efficiency, particularly in scenarios involving repeated computations. We discussed **memoization** as a form of caching used in recursive algorithms and dynamic programming problems to avoid redundant calculations. We also examined various caching strategies for optimizing search and sorting algorithms.

By understanding when and how to apply caching, you can reduce time complexity and make your algorithms significantly faster, particularly for problems with overlapping subproblems, like **Fibonacci numbers** or **tree traversal**. Furthermore, caching plays a critical role in real-world applications like **web services**, **database management**, and **machine learning inference**, helping to optimize performance and ensure faster responses.

CHAPTER 19

PARALLEL PROCESSING AND OPTIMIZING MULTI-THREADED ALGORITHMS

As algorithms grow more complex and datasets increase in size, achieving optimal performance becomes increasingly difficult. One powerful technique for enhancing performance is **parallel processing**, which allows multiple computations to be performed simultaneously across multiple processors or cores. By utilizing **multi-threading**, you can significantly speed up algorithms and make them more efficient, especially for tasks that can be broken down into independent subtasks.

In this chapter, we will cover:

Introduction to parallel processing in algorithms.

How multi-threading can optimize algorithm performance.

Real-world examples: Parallelized searching and sorting.

Tools and frameworks for parallel algorithm implementation.

Introduction to Parallel Processing in Algorithms

Parallel processing refers to the simultaneous execution of multiple tasks or operations. In the context of algorithm optimization, parallel processing enables you to break down a large problem into smaller, independent subtasks that can be executed concurrently. This approach makes it possible to utilize multiple CPU cores, resulting in **significantly reduced execution time** for large-scale problems.

Types of Parallelism:

- **Data Parallelism**: This involves splitting large datasets into smaller chunks, which are processed simultaneously. Each chunk operates independently, and the results are combined at the end.

- **Task Parallelism**: This involves executing different tasks in parallel. These tasks might not be related to a single dataset but can run concurrently to improve overall system performance.

Parallel processing is especially effective for problems where the operations on different pieces of data are independent of each other. In such cases, **multi-threading** (splitting tasks into smaller threads) can be a powerful tool.

Key Benefits of Parallel Processing:

Speedup: By performing multiple tasks simultaneously, parallel processing can reduce the overall time complexity of the algorithm.

Scalability: Parallel algorithms can scale effectively with the number of available CPU cores, leading to linear or even super-linear speedup in ideal cases.

Efficiency: Large computations, like matrix operations or image processing, can be completed more efficiently with parallelism, minimizing the amount of time spent waiting on computations.

How Multi-threading Can Optimize Algorithm Performance

Multi-threading involves dividing an algorithm into smaller threads, each of which can run concurrently. By doing so, multi-threading can drastically speed up certain operations, especially those that involve **independent tasks** or **computations**.

1. Breaking Tasks into Threads

An algorithm that can be divided into **independent tasks** is well-suited for multi-threading. For example:

Independent loops: If a loop operates on data that does not depend on the results of other iterations, each iteration can be performed in a separate thread.

Divide and Conquer Algorithms: Algorithms like **quicksort** and **merge sort** can be parallelized by sorting different parts of the array concurrently.

2. Reducing Bottlenecks

In many cases, multi-threading can help minimize **bottlenecks** that occur when an algorithm performs sequential operations, such as **waiting for I/O operations** or executing long-running computations. By running tasks in parallel, you can maximize CPU utilization and reduce the overall computation time.

3. Shared Resources and Synchronization

While multi-threading provides significant speedups, it can also introduce challenges related to **shared resources** and **synchronization**:

Race Conditions: When multiple threads access shared data, improper handling can lead to inconsistent or incorrect results. This can be mitigated by using **locks**, **semaphores**, or **mutexes** to synchronize access.

Deadlocks: Careful design is necessary to avoid deadlocks, where two or more threads are blocked, waiting for each other indefinitely.

Example: Parallelizing a Simple Task

Let's consider an example where we parallelize a simple **sum** calculation of an array. Without parallelism, the sum function might take longer if the array is large. With multi-threading, we can divide the work into separate chunks, sum them concurrently, and combine the results.

python

```python
import threading

def sum_array(arr, start, end, result, index):
    result[index] = sum(arr[start:end])

def parallel_sum(arr):
    num_threads = 4
    thread_list = []
    result = [0] * num_threads
    chunk_size = len(arr) // num_threads

    # Create threads to compute partial sums
    for i in range(num_threads):
        start = i * chunk_size
```

208

```
        end = (i + 1) * chunk_size if i !=
num_threads - 1 else len(arr)
        thread                           =
threading.Thread(target=sum_array,    args=(arr,
start, end, result, i))
        thread_list.append(thread)
        thread.start()

    # Wait for all threads to finish
    for thread in thread_list:
        thread.join()

    # Combine the partial results
    return sum(result)

# Example usage:
arr = [i for i in range(1000000)]
total_sum = parallel_sum(arr)
print(total_sum)
```

In this example, the array is divided into four chunks, and each chunk is summed concurrently using multiple threads. After all threads complete their work, the partial results are combined to produce the final sum. This approach can be generalized to more complex operations.

Time Complexity of Parallel Sum:

Without parallelism, the time complexity is O(n), where n is the number of elements in the array.

With **four threads**, the time complexity becomes approximately O(n / 4), which speeds up the computation by a factor of four in an ideal scenario (assuming no bottlenecks or synchronization issues).

Real-World Examples: Parallelized Searching and Sorting

1. Parallelized Searching

Search algorithms, like **binary search**, can be parallelized for **large datasets**. For example, in distributed systems or large-scale databases, **parallel search algorithms** can speed up the search process by dividing the dataset into smaller partitions and searching them concurrently.

MapReduce: In large-scale distributed systems (e.g., Hadoop), parallel searching can be done by dividing the dataset into chunks, searching each chunk in parallel, and then aggregating the results.

2. Parallelized Sorting (Merge Sort and Quick Sort)

Sorting algorithms like **merge sort** and **quick sort** can be parallelized by dividing the dataset into smaller subarrays and sorting them concurrently. These algorithms can benefit from parallel processing in both the partitioning and merging phases.

Parallel Merge Sort: In a parallel merge sort, the dataset is divided into smaller chunks that are sorted independently in parallel threads. Afterward, the sorted subarrays are merged together in parallel.

Parallel Quick Sort: Quick sort can also be parallelized by sorting the left and right partitions simultaneously. The pivot selection process can be done sequentially, but the partitioning and sorting of subarrays can occur concurrently.

3. Parallel Searching in Databases

Databases often use parallelized search algorithms to handle large datasets efficiently. For example:

Indexing in databases allows for fast searching by organizing data in a way that reduces search time (e.g., **B-trees**). Parallelizing the search process in these indexes can improve performance when querying large databases.

Tools and Frameworks for Parallel Algorithm Implementation

Several programming languages and frameworks offer built-in tools to make parallel processing easier. These tools abstract much

211

of the complexity associated with thread management, synchronization, and performance tuning.

1. Python: `concurrent.futures` and `threading`

In Python, the **`concurrent.futures`** module provides a simple and high-level interface for parallelism, abstracting away the low-level details of thread management.

Example using `concurrent.futures`:

python

```
from             concurrent.futures            import
ThreadPoolExecutor

def sum_array(arr):
    return sum(arr)

def parallel_sum(arr, num_threads=4):
    chunk_size = len(arr) // num_threads
    with
ThreadPoolExecutor(max_workers=num_threads)    as
executor:
        # Split array into chunks and submit
tasks
        futures = [executor.submit(sum_array,
arr[i * chunk_size:(i + 1) * chunk_size]) for i
in range(num_threads)]
```

```
        results = [future.result() for future in
futures]

    return sum(results)

# Example usage:
arr = [i for i in range(1000000)]
total_sum = parallel_sum(arr)
print(total_sum)
```

> **ThreadPoolExecutor** simplifies the process of managing multiple threads and efficiently distributing tasks across threads.

2. Java: `java.util.concurrent`

In Java, the **`java.util.concurrent`** package provides robust tools for parallelism, including **Executor Services**, **ForkJoinPool**, and **CountDownLatch** for managing multi-threaded tasks.

> **ForkJoinPool**: Specifically designed for **divide and conquer** algorithms, like merge sort and quicksort, to parallelize tasks that can be recursively subdivided.

3. C++: OpenMP and Threading

OpenMP (Open Multi-Processing) is a widely used framework for parallel programming in C++. It allows developers to parallelize loops and other code regions easily by adding compiler directives.

Example using OpenMP:

cpp

```cpp
#include <omp.h>
#include <vector>
#include <iostream>
#include <numeric>

int parallel_sum(const std::vector<int>& arr) {
    int sum = 0;
    #pragma omp parallel for reduction(+:sum)
    for (int i = 0; i < arr.size(); ++i) {
        sum += arr[i];
    }
    return sum;
}

int main() {
    std::vector<int> arr(1000000, 1);   // Array with one million ones
    int total_sum = parallel_sum(arr);
    std::cout << "Total sum: " << total_sum << std::endl;
}
```

OpenMP allows you to parallelize loops with the `#pragma` directive and enables **reduction operations** (like summing an array) in parallel.

Conclusion

In this chapter, we discussed the concept of **parallel processing** and how **multi-threading** can significantly improve the performance of algorithms. We explored several parallelization strategies, including **data parallelism** and **task parallelism**, and how to optimize algorithms like **searching** and **sorting** with parallel techniques.

Real-world examples showed how multi-threading can be applied to speed up operations like searching large datasets or sorting arrays. We also introduced various **tools and frameworks** for implementing parallel algorithms, such as **Python's** `concurrent.futures`, **Java's** `java.util.concurrent`, and **C++'s OpenMP**.

By leveraging these parallel processing tools and strategies, developers can make their algorithms more scalable and efficient, particularly when dealing with large datasets or performance-critical applications.

CHAPTER 20

ALGORITHM OPTIMIZATION IN MACHINE LEARNING

In machine learning (ML), optimizing algorithms is crucial for improving performance, reducing computational costs, and enhancing the overall efficiency of models. Machine learning algorithms often require complex computations, large datasets, and iterative processes that can benefit significantly from algorithmic optimizations. By optimizing algorithms like **gradient descent**, using techniques like **feature selection** and **dimensionality reduction**, and streamlining **training pipelines**, we can improve model performance and reduce training times.

In this chapter, we will cover:

How to optimize algorithms used in machine learning (e.g., gradient descent).

Optimizing training times for deep learning models.

Techniques like feature selection and dimensionality reduction.

Real-world applications: Optimizing machine learning pipelines.

How to Optimize Algorithms Used in Machine Learning (e.g., Gradient Descent)

One of the most common optimization techniques in machine learning is **gradient descent**, which is used to minimize a model's cost function by iteratively updating the model's parameters. Optimizing gradient descent can significantly reduce the time it takes to train models and improve convergence speed.

1. Batch vs. Stochastic vs. Mini-Batch Gradient Descent

Batch Gradient Descent: Computes the gradient of the entire dataset before updating the parameters. This provides an accurate update but can be slow when the dataset is large.

Time Complexity: $O(n)$ for each iteration, where n is the number of training examples.

Pros: Provides accurate updates.

Cons: Slow for large datasets due to the need to process all data points before each update.

Stochastic Gradient Descent (SGD): Computes the gradient using a single training example at a time. This leads to faster updates and helps escape local minima, but can have a lot of variance in the updates.

Time Complexity: O(1) per iteration.

Pros: Faster for large datasets and can escape local minima.

Cons: Noisy updates, which can slow convergence and lead to instability in the learning process.

Mini-Batch Gradient Descent: A hybrid of batch and stochastic gradient descent, mini-batch uses a small subset of the dataset for each update, offering a good balance between speed and accuracy.

Time Complexity: O(m) for each iteration, where m is the mini-batch size.

Pros: Faster convergence and more stable than SGD.

Cons: The performance can still degrade with a very small mini-batch size.

2. Optimizing Learning Rate and Using Adaptive Methods

Choosing the right **learning rate** is crucial for gradient descent optimization. Too small a learning rate can result in slow convergence, while too large a learning rate can lead to overshooting the minimum, making training unstable.

Learning Rate Schedulers: Using a learning rate scheduler that decreases the learning rate over time can help the algorithm converge more effectively.

Example: Learning Rate Scheduling:

```python
import numpy as np

def                    learning_rate_scheduler(epoch,
initial_lr=0.01, decay_rate=0.1):
    return initial_lr * (1 / (1 + decay_rate *
epoch))

# Example usage
epoch = 10
lr = learning_rate_scheduler(epoch)
print(lr)   # Output: 0.009090909090909092
```

Adaptive Gradient Methods:

Adam (Adaptive Moment Estimation) is one of the most popular adaptive gradient methods that combines the benefits of both **Adagrad** and **RMSProp**.

219

RMSProp adjusts the learning rate based on recent gradients, improving convergence speed and stability.

These methods can significantly reduce the time needed to converge and improve the efficiency of the gradient descent process.

3. Momentum and Nesterov Accelerated Gradient (NAG)

Adding **momentum** to gradient descent helps accelerate convergence by adding a fraction of the previous update to the current update, smoothing out oscillations. **Nesterov Accelerated Gradient** (NAG) is a more advanced version of momentum that looks ahead to the next point before updating parameters, often leading to faster convergence.

Momentum Update Formula:

```python
velocity = beta * velocity + (1 - beta) * gradient
parameters = parameters - learning_rate * velocity
```

Pros: Speeds up convergence and improves stability, particularly in regions with shallow gradients.

Optimizing Training Times for Deep Learning Models

Deep learning models, especially **neural networks**, can take a long time to train, particularly with large datasets. There are several techniques that can be used to speed up the training process.

1. Parallel and Distributed Training

Training deep learning models on a single machine with large datasets can be slow. To optimize training time, you can parallelize the training process by utilizing multiple CPUs or GPUs.

- **Data Parallelism**: Distributes the data across multiple processors, where each processor computes the gradients for a subset of the data.

- **Model Parallelism**: Distributes the model itself across different devices, which is useful for very large models.

- **Distributed Training Frameworks**: Frameworks like **TensorFlow**, **PyTorch**, and **Horovod** support distributed training, enabling faster training on multiple GPUs or nodes.

2. Using Pre-trained Models

Instead of training a deep learning model from scratch, **transfer learning** can be used to fine-tune pre-trained models. This significantly reduces training time, as the model has already learned many useful features on a large dataset, and you only need to fine-tune it for your specific task.

> **Example**: Fine-tuning a **pre-trained ResNet** or **VGG** model on a new dataset can reduce training time from weeks to just hours.

3. Batch Normalization

Batch normalization normalizes the inputs to each layer in the network, which helps to reduce training time and improve convergence speed. By maintaining a stable distribution of activations, batch normalization allows for higher learning rates and faster convergence.

Benefits:

Reduces the internal covariate shift.

Acts as a regularizer, reducing the need for Dropout.

4. Gradient Clipping

Gradient clipping prevents the gradients from becoming too large and causing the model to explode. This is particularly important in **Recurrent Neural Networks (RNNs)**, where gradients can become very large during backpropagation.

Example: Clipping gradients in PyTorch:

```python
torch.nn.utils.clip_grad_norm_(model.parameters
(), max_norm=1.0)
```

This technique ensures that the gradients stay within a specified range, preventing them from becoming too large and destabilizing training.

Techniques Like Feature Selection and Dimensionality Reduction

When working with high-dimensional data, reducing the number of features or dimensions can significantly speed up training time and reduce overfitting. Two common techniques for dimensionality reduction are **feature selection** and **principal component analysis (PCA)**.

223

1. Feature Selection

Feature selection involves selecting a subset of relevant features from the original dataset. This reduces the computational cost and potentially improves model performance by removing irrelevant or redundant features.

> **Filter Methods**: These involve selecting features based on statistical measures, like correlation or mutual information, that show how strongly a feature is related to the target variable.

> **Wrapper Methods**: These involve using a machine learning algorithm to evaluate the performance of feature subsets and selecting the best-performing subset.

> **Embedded Methods**: These use algorithms like **Lasso regression** or **decision trees** that perform feature selection during the model training process.

2. Principal Component Analysis (PCA)

PCA is a popular dimensionality reduction technique that transforms data into a smaller set of linearly uncorrelated components. By keeping only the most significant components, PCA reduces the number of dimensions without losing too much information.

Example of PCA:

python

```
from sklearn.decomposition import PCA

pca = PCA(n_components=2)
X_reduced = pca.fit_transform(X)   # Reduce the
dataset X to 2 dimensions
```

PCA can help speed up the training process by reducing the number of features while retaining as much variance as possible.

Real-World Applications: Optimizing ML Pipelines

Optimizing machine learning algorithms is not limited to the model training process but extends to the entire **ML pipeline**, which involves data preprocessing, model training, and evaluation. Here are a few ways to optimize the entire pipeline:

1. Data Preprocessing Optimization

Data Augmentation: In domains like image processing, **data augmentation** techniques like rotation, scaling, and flipping can create new data points without requiring additional computation. This can help improve model generalization.

Efficient Data Loading: Use **data generators** or **dataloader frameworks** that load batches of data efficiently from disk to reduce I/O bottlenecks during training.

2. Hyperparameter Tuning

Efficient hyperparameter tuning can drastically improve model performance. Techniques like **grid search** and **random search** can be used, but **Bayesian optimization** and **genetic algorithms** can provide better results with fewer iterations, reducing computational cost.

3. Model Ensembling

Instead of training one model, combining the predictions of multiple models (using techniques like **bagging**, **boosting**, or **stacking**) can improve accuracy. However, ensembling can be computationally expensive. Optimizing ensembling methods (e.g., using fewer base models or combining the best-performing models) can speed up predictions without sacrificing too much performance.

Conclusion

In this chapter, we explored various strategies for optimizing machine learning algorithms. We discussed how **gradient descent** and **multi-threading** can speed up model training, and how techniques like **feature selection** and **PCA** can reduce training times by simplifying the problem space.

We also examined ways to optimize the **training times for deep learning models** using techniques like **parallel processing, pre-trained models**, and **batch normalization**. Additionally, we looked at how to optimize the entire **machine learning pipeline**, from data preprocessing to hyperparameter tuning, ensuring that your ML models are not only accurate but also efficient.

By leveraging these optimization techniques, you can build machine learning models that are faster to train, more scalable, and better suited to handle large datasets, ultimately improving both the performance and practicality of your ML systems.

CHAPTER 21

NETWORK OPTIMIZATION ALGORITHMS

In today's connected world, **network optimization** plays a crucial role in ensuring that data flows efficiently across communication networks, whether it's the **internet, corporate networks**, or **telecommunication systems**. Optimization algorithms are used to solve a variety of problems related to **routing, traffic flow**, and **bandwidth allocation**, all of which are fundamental to enhancing the performance, reliability, and scalability of networks.

In this chapter, we will cover:

Introduction to network optimization problems.

Algorithms for routing, traffic flow, and bandwidth allocation.

Example: Optimizing packet routing with Dijkstra's algorithm.

Real-world use case: Network load balancing and optimization.

Introduction to Network Optimization Problems

Network optimization involves improving the performance of a network by ensuring efficient use of resources such as bandwidth, routes, and traffic. Some of the common optimization problems in networking include:

Routing: Finding the most efficient path between two nodes in a network.

Traffic Flow: Ensuring that data packets can move smoothly through the network without congestion.

Bandwidth Allocation: Distributing bandwidth across different users or applications in a way that maximizes network efficiency.

Network Design: Ensuring the network is structured in a way that maximizes efficiency and reliability while minimizing costs.

These problems typically arise in both **wired** and **wireless networks**, and solving them efficiently requires advanced algorithms. The goal is to minimize delays, maximize throughput, reduce congestion, and ensure the overall reliability of the network.

Algorithms for Routing, Traffic Flow, and Bandwidth Allocation

Various algorithms have been developed to solve network optimization problems, including those for routing, traffic management, and bandwidth allocation. Let's discuss some of these core algorithms:

1. Routing Algorithms

Routing is the process of determining the path for data to travel from the source to the destination across a network. The choice of the routing algorithm impacts network efficiency, reliability, and scalability.

> **Shortest Path Algorithms**: These algorithms calculate the shortest or most efficient route between two points in a network. Some commonly used shortest path algorithms include:
>
> > **Dijkstra's Algorithm**: Calculates the shortest path from a source node to all other nodes in a graph, making it ideal for **weighted graphs**.
> >
> > **Bellman-Ford Algorithm**: Similar to Dijkstra's, but can handle negative edge weights.

A Algorithm*: An extension of Dijkstra's that uses heuristics to speed up the search for the shortest path.

Flooding: A technique where packets are sent to every neighboring node until they reach the destination. This is simple but inefficient in large networks.

Routing Protocols: In large-scale networks like the **internet**, algorithms are implemented via protocols such as **OSPF (Open Shortest Path First)**, **BGP (Border Gateway Protocol)**, and **RIP (Routing Information Protocol)**.

2. Traffic Flow Optimization

Traffic flow optimization refers to techniques that ensure efficient movement of data across a network. This involves managing data traffic in such a way that minimizes congestion and delays. Key strategies include:

Flow Control: Managing the rate at which data packets are sent to ensure that routers and switches don't become overloaded.

Congestion Avoidance: Using algorithms like **TCP congestion control** (e.g., **TCP Reno**, **TCP Vegas**) to detect and avoid congestion in the network by adjusting the rate of packet transmission.

Load **Balancing**: Distributing the network traffic evenly across multiple paths or servers to avoid overloading any single resource.

3. Bandwidth Allocation

Bandwidth allocation involves distributing available bandwidth across different users, devices, or services. Efficient allocation ensures that data can be transferred without delays while making the best use of the available resources.

Quality of Service (QoS): QoS algorithms prioritize certain types of traffic (e.g., video streaming) over others (e.g., emails) to ensure that critical services receive the required bandwidth.

Fairness Algorithms: These algorithms ensure that resources are allocated fairly among users. Techniques like **TCP Fairness** and **Max-Min Fairness** are often used in resource-sharing scenarios.

Traffic Shaping: Regulating the flow of data to smooth out traffic patterns and ensure optimal bandwidth usage.

Example: Optimizing Packet Routing with Dijkstra's Algorithm

Dijkstra's Algorithm is one of the most widely used algorithms for routing in **weighted graphs**, such as computer networks. It calculates the shortest path from a source node to all other nodes in the network, ensuring that data is sent along the most efficient route, minimizing delays.

Steps in Dijkstra's Algorithm:

Initialization: Set the initial distance to all nodes to infinity, except for the source node, which is set to zero.

Processing Nodes: Visit each node, updating the shortest distance to its neighboring nodes.

Selecting the Node with the Smallest Distance: After each iteration, select the node with the smallest tentative distance and mark it as visited.

Repeat Until All Nodes are Visited: Continue this process until all nodes have been visited.

Example of Dijkstra's Algorithm in Python:

```python
python

import heapq

def dijkstra(graph, start):
    # Initialize the distances and priority queue
    distances = {node: float('infinity') for node
in graph}
```

```
    distances[start] = 0
    pq = [(0, start)]  # (distance, node)

    while pq:
        current_distance,    current_node    =
heapq.heappop(pq)

        if            current_distance            >
distances[current_node]:
            continue

        for       neighbor,       weight       in
graph[current_node].items():
            distance = current_distance + weight

            if distance < distances[neighbor]:
                distances[neighbor] = distance
                heapq.heappush(pq,      (distance,
neighbor))

    return distances

# Example graph (adjacency list representation)
graph = {
    'A': {'B': 1, 'C': 4},
    'B': {'A': 1, 'C': 2, 'D': 5},
    'C': {'A': 4, 'B': 2, 'D': 1},
    'D': {'B': 5, 'C': 1}
}
```

```
print(dijkstra(graph, 'A'))   # Output: {'A': 0,
'B': 1, 'C': 3, 'D': 4}
```

In this example, Dijkstra's algorithm is used to calculate the shortest path from node A to all other nodes in the graph. The output shows the minimum distance to each node from A.

Time Complexity:

Time Complexity: O(E log V), where E is the number of edges and V is the number of vertices in the graph.

Space Complexity: O(V), for storing distances and the priority queue.

Real-World Use Case: Network Load Balancing and Optimization

Network load balancing is the process of distributing network traffic across multiple servers or paths to ensure no single server or path becomes overwhelmed. Load balancing optimizes network performance, reduces congestion, and improves system reliability.

1. Load Balancing Algorithms

Some common algorithms used for load balancing include:

Round-Robin: Requests are distributed sequentially across all servers. This is simple but does not account for the current load on each server.

Least Connections: New requests are sent to the server with the fewest active connections. This method works well when the servers have varying processing power or when load varies between requests.

Weighted Round-Robin: Servers are assigned weights based on their capacity. Servers with higher weights handle more traffic.

Least Response Time: Requests are routed to the server with the fastest response time.

2. Dynamic Load Balancing

For large-scale distributed systems, **dynamic load balancing** continuously adjusts how traffic is distributed based on real-time data. It can account for changes in server load, network conditions, and resource availability.

Example: In **cloud computing**, load balancing is used to distribute requests across multiple virtual machines (VMs) or containers to ensure no individual VM becomes overwhelmed. This optimizes resource usage and ensures high availability.

3. Software and Hardware Load Balancers

Load balancing can be achieved through both **software-based** and **hardware-based** solutions:

Software Load Balancers: These are typically implemented as part of the network software stack and can be configured to suit specific needs (e.g., **Nginx, HAProxy**).

Hardware Load Balancers: These dedicated devices are designed to manage large-scale network traffic and are often used in enterprise environments.

Example: Cloud-based Load Balancing

In a **cloud computing environment**, such as with **Amazon Web Services (AWS)**, load balancing is performed automatically through services like **Elastic Load Balancing (ELB)**. The load balancer monitors the health of instances and routes traffic only to healthy instances, ensuring optimal resource usage.

Conclusion

In this chapter, we explored the importance of **network optimization** and discussed various algorithms for optimizing routing, traffic flow, and bandwidth allocation. We detailed **Dijkstra's algorithm** as an example of optimizing packet routing in a network, showing how it can be used to determine the shortest path in a graph efficiently.

We also discussed **network load balancing** and optimization, which are essential for ensuring the smooth flow of traffic across a network while minimizing congestion and downtime. Finally, we looked at real-world use cases where network optimization techniques, including **load balancing** and **traffic management**, are applied to ensure high performance and reliability in distributed systems.

By understanding these network optimization algorithms, you can improve the efficiency and performance of communication networks, whether for **internet routing**, **data center management**, or **cloud computing environments**.

CHAPTER 22

OPTIMIZING SEARCH ALGORITHMS FOR LARGE-SCALE DATA

As the amount of data grows exponentially, efficiently searching through large datasets becomes a significant challenge. Optimizing search algorithms is crucial for ensuring fast query responses, especially in systems where data is distributed across multiple servers or stored in complex structures. In this chapter, we will explore strategies to optimize search algorithms for large-scale data, focusing on techniques like **indexing** and **data partitioning**. We'll also cover real-world examples of search optimizations in **distributed databases** and applications like **full-text search** and **indexing**.

In this chapter, we will cover:

Searching through large datasets efficiently.

Optimizing search algorithms using indexing and data partitioning.

Example: Search optimizations in distributed databases.

Real-world applications: Full-text search and indexing in large systems.

Searching Through Large Datasets Efficiently

When dealing with **large datasets**, traditional search methods, like **linear search**, become inefficient due to their time complexity of O(n). For large datasets, more advanced algorithms and data structures are required to make searches more efficient.

1. Divide and Conquer Approach

The **divide and conquer** strategy, where a dataset is divided into smaller parts and each part is processed independently, is often used to improve search efficiency. One of the most famous examples of this is **binary search** on **sorted** data, which has a time complexity of O(log n).

2. Search Trees

Binary Search Trees (BST): A binary search tree is a data structure where each node has two children: a left child containing smaller values and a right child containing larger values. Searching in a balanced binary search tree has a time complexity of O(log n), but this can degrade to O(n) if the tree is unbalanced.

Balanced Search Trees: To avoid the worst-case time complexity of O(n), self-balancing trees like **AVL trees** and **Red-Black trees** ensure that the height of the tree remains logarithmic. This guarantees efficient search operations even with a large dataset.

B-Trees and B+ Trees: These are generalized binary search trees designed to work efficiently on disk storage, typically used in **databases** and **file systems**.

3. Hashing

Hashing is a technique that uses a hash function to map data to specific indices in a hash table, enabling **constant time (O(1))** lookups. However, hashing may not always be suitable for range queries or ordered searches, making it more appropriate for applications like **dictionary lookups** and **set membership testing**.

Optimizing Search Algorithms Using Indexing and Data Partitioning

As datasets grow, **indexing** and **data partitioning** become crucial for improving search performance. These techniques allow for faster search times by organizing the data in such a way that queries can be answered more efficiently.

1. Indexing

Indexing is the process of creating a data structure that allows for fast searching of specific data. Indexes are typically built using search trees, hash tables, or inverted indexes.

> **B-Tree Indexes**: Common in relational databases, **B-Trees** organize data in a way that minimizes the number of disk accesses required to find an element. Searching, insertion, and deletion all have a time complexity of $O(\log n)$ due to the balanced nature of the tree.

> **Inverted Indexes**: Frequently used in **full-text search** systems, an inverted index maps each word to the documents or data entries that contain it. This allows for fast retrieval of documents that contain specific keywords.

> **Composite Indexes**: In databases, a **composite index** allows for indexing on multiple columns, enabling multi-attribute searches without having to scan the entire dataset.

2. Data Partitioning

Data partitioning involves dividing large datasets into smaller, more manageable pieces, which can be processed in parallel or distributed across multiple machines.

Horizontal Partitioning (Sharding): In horizontal partitioning, a large dataset is split into smaller, more manageable chunks called **shards**. Each shard contains a subset of the data, which can be distributed across different servers or databases. This approach is commonly used in distributed databases, where each shard is independently queried.

Vertical Partitioning: Instead of splitting rows, vertical partitioning splits the columns of the data. This is useful when certain columns are queried more frequently than others.

Range-based Partitioning: Data is divided based on certain ranges, such as numeric or alphabetical ranges. This partitioning method is useful when queries often ask for data within specific ranges, like retrieving records for a certain date range or price range.

Hash-based Partitioning: Data is divided using a hash function applied to the data. This ensures an even distribution of data across the partitions, which helps balance the load on each partition.

Example: Search Optimizations in Distributed Databases

Distributed databases often involve partitioning data across multiple machines, and optimizing search in such systems

243

requires specialized algorithms to minimize latency and ensure quick retrieval. One of the most important techniques for optimizing search in distributed databases is **sharding**.

Sharding splits a large dataset into smaller, more manageable pieces (shards), and these shards can be distributed across multiple servers. This allows for parallel processing, faster query execution, and better utilization of resources.

1. Search in a Sharded Database

In a sharded database, searching involves querying the relevant shard(s) based on the data partitioning strategy. For example, if the data is partitioned by **user ID**, and a query is searching for a specific user, the system can route the query directly to the shard containing that user's data, avoiding the need to scan the entire dataset.

Data Locality: When data is partitioned effectively, queries that access a single shard can be executed more quickly because the dataset is localized to a specific server.

Distributed Indexing: Indexes can be distributed across shards, enabling efficient search queries within each shard. In some cases, global indexes can be maintained to facilitate cross-shard searches.

2. Search Across Multiple Shards

In cases where a query needs to access multiple shards (for example, a query that spans multiple ranges), the system uses **distributed query processing** to send the query to the appropriate shards in parallel. After each shard executes its part of the query, the results are aggregated and returned to the user.

Query Routing: Distributed databases use **query routing** algorithms to direct queries to the appropriate shards based on the partitioning key.

Consistency Models: Many distributed databases implement consistency models such as **Eventual Consistency** or **Strong Consistency**, which must be factored into the search optimization process.

Real-World Applications: Full-Text Search and Indexing in Large Systems

One of the most common and powerful use cases for **indexing** and search optimization is **full-text search**. Full-text search allows users to search for documents or content based on keywords or phrases, and it relies heavily on efficient indexing techniques.

1. Full-Text Search with Inverted Indexes

In full-text search, an **inverted index** is used to map each word in a collection of documents to the list of documents that contain it. When a user performs a search, the search engine can quickly find which documents contain the relevant keywords by looking up the terms in the index, rather than scanning every document.

> **Example**: Search engines like **Google** and **Elasticsearch** use inverted indexes to enable fast, scalable full-text searches over massive datasets.

2. Optimizing Full-Text Search with Caching

To further optimize performance, full-text search systems often employ **caching** strategies to store frequently accessed documents or search results. This reduces the need to re-query the database for commonly searched terms, providing faster response times.

3. Distributed Search Engines

In distributed search engines, the data is often partitioned and indexed across multiple machines. **Apache Solr** and **Elasticsearch** are two popular systems that support distributed indexing, allowing for fast searches across large datasets that are distributed across many nodes.

Sharding in Search Engines: Both **Solr** and **Elasticsearch** use sharding to divide the index into smaller chunks, which are distributed across multiple servers. This enables parallel processing and faster query execution.

Replication for High Availability: Distributed search systems often replicate data to ensure high availability and fault tolerance. This ensures that even if one shard or node fails, the system can continue functioning by serving results from replicated copies of the index.

Conclusion

In this chapter, we explored the challenges and techniques involved in **optimizing search algorithms for large-scale data**. We discussed how search algorithms can be optimized through **indexing** and **data partitioning**. By leveraging techniques such as **binary search trees, hashing**, and **distributed indexing**, we can significantly improve the efficiency of search queries on large datasets.

We also examined the use of **sharding** in **distributed databases**, allowing for faster, parallelized queries across large datasets. In real-world applications, **full-text search** and **indexing** are critical for ensuring fast, efficient searches in systems like search engines and document databases.

By implementing these search optimization strategies, we can achieve faster query responses, better resource utilization, and improved scalability in large-scale data systems. Whether you're working on distributed databases, search engines, or other data-intensive applications, optimizing search algorithms is key to building high-performance, efficient systems.

CHAPTER 23

ALGORITHMS FOR REAL-TIME SYSTEMS AND OPTIMIZATIONS

Real-time systems are critical to applications where timely and predictable responses are essential. These systems include embedded devices, industrial control systems, telecommunications, video streaming, and autonomous vehicles, among others. Designing and optimizing algorithms for these applications is challenging because they need to meet strict requirements for **latency, throughput**, and **reliability**. The goal of optimization in real-time systems is to ensure that tasks are completed within their time constraints without overloading system resources.

In this chapter, we will cover:

Challenges in real-time systems.

How to design and optimize algorithms for real-time applications.

Example: Scheduling algorithms in operating systems.

Optimizing for low-latency and high-throughput systems.

Challenges in Real-Time Systems

Real-time systems are unique because they need to operate within **strict timing constraints**. These constraints are typically classified into two categories:

- **Hard Real-Time Systems**: These systems have rigid deadlines. Missing a deadline results in a failure, which could lead to disastrous consequences, as in the case of safety-critical applications like **airbag systems** or **medical devices**.

- **Soft Real-Time Systems**: These systems can tolerate some level of delay. Missing a deadline doesn't cause catastrophic failure, but performance is still degraded, as seen in **video streaming** or **multimedia processing**.

Key Challenges in Real-Time Systems:

- **Time Constraints**: The most pressing issue in real-time systems is ensuring that tasks are completed within their allocated time frame. These systems often involve managing multiple tasks concurrently, each with different priorities and deadlines.

- **Concurrency**: Real-time systems often need to handle multiple tasks or events simultaneously, making concurrency a significant challenge. Proper synchronization and scheduling are necessary to avoid race conditions and ensure tasks are executed in a timely manner.

Resource Constraints: Real-time systems often operate with limited resources (CPU, memory, bandwidth). Efficient management of these resources is crucial to meeting real-time constraints.

Deterministic Behavior: Real-time systems must guarantee that their behavior is predictable. This includes having predictable latencies, bounded execution times, and reliable task completion.

How to Design and Optimize Algorithms for Real-Time Applications

Designing algorithms for real-time systems requires careful consideration of time constraints, system resources, and the need for concurrency. The goal is to ensure that tasks are executed in a way that meets deadlines and guarantees system stability.

1. Task Scheduling Algorithms

Scheduling is at the heart of real-time systems, as it determines the order in which tasks are executed. There are several approaches to scheduling, each with its own strengths and trade-offs.

Preemptive vs. Non-Preemptive Scheduling:

Preemptive Scheduling: Allows tasks to be interrupted and resumed later, ensuring that higher-priority tasks can be executed immediately. This is useful in systems with varying task priorities.

Non-Preemptive Scheduling: Once a task starts executing, it runs to completion. This method is simpler but can lead to poor responsiveness in systems where higher-priority tasks need to interrupt lower-priority ones.

2. Priority-Based Scheduling

In **priority-based scheduling**, each task is assigned a priority, and tasks with higher priority are executed first. This is particularly useful for hard real-time systems where deadlines must be met.

Fixed Priority Scheduling: Tasks are assigned fixed priorities, and tasks with higher priorities are executed first. Popular fixed priority algorithms include:

Rate-Monotonic Scheduling (RMS): Assigns tasks priorities based on their period (time between recurring executions). The task with the shortest period gets the highest priority.

Deadline-Monotonic Scheduling (DMS): Tasks with the nearest deadline get the highest priority.

Dynamic Priority Scheduling: Tasks are dynamically prioritized based on certain criteria, such as deadlines or execution times. Common dynamic priority algorithms include:

Earliest Deadline First (EDF): A dynamic priority scheduling algorithm where tasks with the earliest deadline are given the highest priority. EDF guarantees optimal performance for soft real-time systems.

Least Laxity First (LLF): The task with the least amount of slack time (time remaining before a task's deadline) is executed next.

3. Round-Robin Scheduling for Soft Real-Time Systems

For soft real-time systems where deadlines can be missed without catastrophic results, **round-robin scheduling** can be used. In round-robin scheduling, each task is given a fixed time slice or quantum to execute. If a task doesn't finish within its time slice, it is preempted and placed back in the queue. This ensures that all tasks get a fair share of CPU time and can be suitable for systems that require **fairness** but don't have rigid deadlines.

253

4. Resource Allocation and Locking

In real-time systems, managing shared resources (e.g., memory, CPU) is crucial to avoid **deadlocks** and **race conditions**. Algorithms like **priority inheritance** and **priority ceiling protocols** ensure that higher-priority tasks can access shared resources without interference from lower-priority tasks, minimizing the chance of deadlocks and ensuring timely execution.

Example: Scheduling Algorithms in Operating Systems

One of the most common real-time system components is the **operating system (OS)**, which needs to manage multiple processes or threads, ensuring that high-priority tasks meet their deadlines. Let's explore a popular scheduling algorithm: **Rate-Monotonic Scheduling (RMS)**.

Rate-Monotonic Scheduling (RMS)

Rate-Monotonic Scheduling assigns higher priorities to tasks with shorter periods (i.e., tasks that need to execute more frequently). This algorithm is optimal for fixed-priority preemptive scheduling in real-time systems, and it ensures that the system can handle periodic tasks with predictable execution times.

Time Complexity: The time complexity of RMS is generally $O(n \log n)$ for scheduling n tasks, as it requires sorting the tasks by their period.

Example of RMS in an OS:

Suppose we have three tasks with the following periods and execution times:

Task 1: Period = 4ms, Execution time = 2ms

Task 2: Period = 6ms, Execution time = 3ms

Task 3: Period = 8ms, Execution time = 4ms

In RMS, Task 1 will have the highest priority, followed by Task 2 and Task 3. The operating system will schedule Task 1 first, then Task 2, and finally Task 3, ensuring that each task completes its execution within its period.

Challenges: RMS works well when tasks are independent and can run to completion within their respective periods. However, it may not work optimally if tasks have varying resource requirements or need to interact with other processes.

Optimizing for Low-Latency and High-Throughput Systems

Optimizing real-time systems for **low-latency** and **high-throughput** is essential in applications like high-frequency trading, video streaming, and telecommunication. Here are some strategies:

1. Low-Latency Systems

Low-latency systems aim to minimize the delay between input and output, which is critical in applications like **online gaming**, **video conferencing**, and **autonomous driving**.

> **Preemptive Scheduling**: Preemptive scheduling ensures that high-priority tasks can interrupt lower-priority tasks, minimizing the response time for critical tasks.

> **Interrupt Handling**: Efficient interrupt handling can minimize the time it takes to process external events, which is crucial in systems that need to react to inputs in real-time.

2. High-Throughput Systems

In **high-throughput systems**, the goal is to process as many tasks or data points as possible within a given time frame, making it ideal for applications like **data streaming**, **network packet processing**, and **data analytics**.

Parallel Processing: By using **multi-threading** or **multi-core processors**, high-throughput systems can execute multiple tasks concurrently, significantly improving throughput.

Load Balancing: Efficient load balancing algorithms ensure that system resources are used optimally, distributing the workload evenly across multiple processors or servers.

Conclusion

In this chapter, we explored the key principles of **algorithm optimization for real-time systems**. We discussed the challenges in real-time systems, such as ensuring predictable timing and handling concurrency, and we covered **scheduling algorithms** like **Rate-Monotonic Scheduling** and **Earliest Deadline First** that ensure tasks are executed within their time constraints. We also examined optimization techniques for **low-latency** and **high-throughput** systems, which are critical for applications like video streaming, online gaming, and high-frequency trading.

Optimizing real-time systems involves a careful balance between **timing constraints**, **resource management**, and **algorithmic efficiency**. By understanding the trade-offs and selecting the appropriate algorithms for specific real-time applications, you can build systems that meet the strict requirements for latency, throughput, and reliability.

CHAPTER 24

OPTIMIZING ALGORITHMIC COMPLEXITY IN COMPETITIVE PROGRAMMING

In **competitive programming**, the goal is to solve problems efficiently within a strict time limit. Since many problems involve large datasets or require complex operations, optimizing the **algorithmic complexity** is crucial for success. Understanding and applying strategies to reduce time and space complexity can help you tackle challenges more effectively and outpace your competitors.

In this chapter, we will cover:

Strategies for reducing algorithmic complexity in contests.

Common optimization tricks for competitive programmers.

Example: Optimizing graph traversal for time-sensitive problems.

Tips for efficient problem-solving in competitive coding.

Strategies for Reducing Algorithmic Complexity in Contests

When participating in programming contests, time is of the essence. Therefore, understanding how to optimize your code for both **time complexity** and **space complexity** is essential. Here are some strategies to help you reduce algorithmic complexity:

1. Preprocessing the Data

For many problems, **preprocessing** the input data can save time during the actual computation. By performing one-time operations before the core logic of the algorithm, you can reduce redundant calculations.

- **Sorting**: Sorting the input data may allow you to use more efficient algorithms (e.g., binary search) that reduce time complexity.

- **Prefix and Suffix Arrays**: For problems involving cumulative sums or products, **prefix arrays** (or **suffix arrays**) can help reduce the time complexity of repeated calculations.

- **Precomputing Results**: In some problems, you may precompute solutions for smaller subproblems and store the results to avoid recalculating them later (e.g., **dynamic programming**).

2. Using More Efficient Data Structures

Choosing the right data structure can significantly reduce the time complexity of your algorithm. In competitive programming, you should be familiar with various data structures and understand how to choose the best one for a given problem.

>   **Heaps**: If you need to frequently access the maximum or minimum element, a **heap** (priority queue) provides O(log n) access time for insertion and deletion, which is faster than searching a list or array.

>   **Hash Maps**: For problems that involve frequent lookups or checking set membership, **hash maps** (or hash sets) offer constant time O(1) complexity on average for insertion, deletion, and lookups.

>   **Segment Trees and Fenwick Trees**: For range queries and updates, **segment trees** or **Fenwick trees** (binary indexed trees) allow for efficient O(log n) time complexity.

3. Greedy Algorithms

Greedy algorithms work by making locally optimal choices at each step with the hope of finding a global optimum. Often, these algorithms provide efficient solutions to problems that would otherwise require more complex algorithms.

Example: For problems like **activity selection** or **minimum spanning tree** (using **Prim's** or **Kruskal's** algorithm), greedy algorithms can provide O(n log n) solutions, which are far better than the $O(n^2)$ alternatives.

4. Dividing the Problem (Divide and Conquer)

When faced with a problem that has repetitive subproblems, **divide and conquer** techniques can help break the problem down into smaller, manageable parts. This approach can help reduce time complexity by eliminating redundant computations and using efficient recursive solutions.

Example: Algorithms like **merge sort** (O(n log n)) and **quick sort** (O(n log n) on average) are based on the divide and conquer paradigm and perform better than simple $O(n^2)$ sorting algorithms.

5. Avoiding Nested Loops

Nested loops can quickly lead to exponential or polynomial time complexity ($O(n^2)$, $O(n^3)$, etc.). A common optimization trick is to try to avoid using nested loops where possible. Consider using more efficient data structures or algorithms to reduce the need for nested iterations.

Example: Instead of iterating over all pairs of elements in a list, consider using a hash set or hash map to keep track of previously seen values for a faster solution.

Common Optimization Tricks for Competitive Programmers

Here are some common optimization tricks that competitive programmers often use to improve algorithmic efficiency:

1. Binary Search

When a problem involves finding an element in a sorted array or checking for a condition within a range, **binary search** can reduce the time complexity from $O(n)$ to $O(\log n)$. Binary search can also be used for **searching in sorted or monotonic sequences**.

Example: Instead of searching for a target element linearly, use binary search to find the element in $O(\log n)$ time in a sorted array.

2. Sliding Window Technique

The sliding window technique is useful when solving problems that require examining subarrays or subsequences. Instead of recalculating the result for each new window from scratch, you can "slide" the window by adjusting the left and right boundaries, maintaining the state of the current window in constant time.

Example: Finding the maximum sum of a subarray of fixed size (size k) can be optimized using a sliding window approach, reducing the time complexity from O(n * k) to O(n).

3. Union-Find (Disjoint Set Union)

The **Union-Find** (also known as **Disjoint Set Union, DSU**) data structure is highly effective for handling problems involving connected components, such as finding cycles in a graph or determining the connectedness of nodes.

Optimization: Using **path compression** and **union by rank** helps keep the time complexity nearly constant, specifically $O(\alpha(n))$ (where α is the inverse Ackermann function).

4. Memoization

Memoization is a technique where you store the results of expensive function calls and reuse them when the same inputs occur again. This technique is commonly used in **dynamic programming** problems and can reduce the time complexity from exponential to polynomial in many cases.

Example: In the Fibonacci sequence, instead of calculating each Fibonacci number recursively, memoization stores previously computed values to avoid redundant calculations.

5. Bit Manipulation

Bit manipulation allows you to operate on numbers at the binary level, which can be much faster and more efficient than regular arithmetic operations. Common techniques include using **bitwise AND, OR, XOR**, and **shifting** to solve problems related to **sets**, **subsets**, and **combinations**.

> **Example**: In problems involving subsets or powers of 2, bit manipulation can reduce the time complexity and avoid the use of nested loops.

Example: Optimizing Graph Traversal for Time-Sensitive Problems

In many graph-related problems, traversal is key to solving the problem. Two common graph traversal algorithms are **Depth-First Search (DFS)** and **Breadth-First Search (BFS)**. Let's explore an optimization strategy for **BFS** when dealing with time-sensitive problems.

1. Optimizing BFS with Early Stopping

In problems where you only need to find the shortest path or reach a specific node in the graph, there is no need to continue the traversal once the target is found. By using an **early stopping** condition, you can avoid unnecessary operations and reduce runtime.

Example: Finding the Shortest Path in an Unweighted Graph:

python

```python
from collections import deque

def bfs_optimized(graph, start, target):
    visited = set()
    queue = deque([start])
    visited.add(start)

    while queue:
        node = queue.popleft()
        if node == target:
            return True  # Early stopping

        for neighbor in graph[node]:
            if neighbor not in visited:
                visited.add(neighbor)
                queue.append(neighbor)
    return False

# Example usage
graph = {
    0: [1, 2],
    1: [0, 3, 4],
```

```
    2: [0],
    3: [1],
    4: [1]
}
print(bfs_optimized(graph, 0, 4))  # Output: True
```

In this case, the search stops as soon as the target node is found, improving efficiency in time-sensitive problems.

Tips for Efficient Problem-Solving in Competitive Coding

To excel in competitive programming, it's not only important to have a solid understanding of algorithms but also to be able to apply efficient problem-solving strategies under time pressure. Here are some tips for efficient problem-solving:

1. Understand the Problem First

Before jumping into coding, carefully read and understand the problem. Identify the input, output, constraints, and edge cases. Once you have a clear understanding of the problem, you can choose the right approach to solve it efficiently.

2. Start with a Brute Force Solution

In some cases, starting with a brute-force approach can help you understand the problem better. Once you have a working solution, you can then focus on optimizing it.

3. Focus on Time and Space Complexity

Always keep an eye on the algorithm's time and space complexity. For large datasets or constraints, ensure that your algorithm will run within the given limits. Avoid algorithms with time complexities of $O(n^2)$ or $O(n^3)$ unless the problem allows it.

4. Practice and Learn from Others

The best way to improve your competitive programming skills is through practice. Regularly solve problems on platforms like **LeetCode**, **Codeforces**, and **AtCoder**. Also, analyze the solutions of other top programmers to learn new techniques and optimization tricks.

5. Don't Over-Optimize Early

In competitive programming, you may feel pressured to optimize every line of code from the start. However, it's important to first implement a working solution, then optimize it only if necessary. Over-optimizing early can waste valuable time.

Conclusion

In this chapter, we explored strategies for **optimizing algorithmic complexity** in **competitive programming**. We discussed common optimization techniques such as **preprocessing, efficient data structures, greedy algorithms, divide and**

conquer, and **search optimizations**. We also looked at specific examples like optimizing **graph traversal** for time-sensitive problems and discussed tips for efficient problem-solving under contest conditions.

By mastering these techniques and continuously practicing, you can enhance your ability to solve problems efficiently and improve your performance in competitive programming contests.

CHAPTER 25

MEMORY-OPTIMIZED ALGORITHMS FOR EMBEDDED SYSTEMS

Embedded systems are designed to perform specific tasks with limited computational resources, including constrained memory, processing power, and energy. In these systems, memory optimization is not just a performance issue but a fundamental requirement for ensuring that the device can operate efficiently without running out of memory. The goal is to design algorithms that use as little memory as possible while still providing the required functionality.

In this chapter, we will cover:

Designing algorithms for low-memory devices.

Memory optimization techniques for embedded systems.

Example: Data compression and optimization algorithms for limited memory.

Real-world use cases: Mobile apps, IoT, and embedded systems.

Designing Algorithms for Low-Memory Devices

When designing algorithms for **embedded systems**, the primary goal is to minimize the memory footprint while ensuring that the system remains functional and responsive. To achieve this, designers must make careful choices about the data structures and algorithms they use, focusing on memory efficiency and minimizing overhead.

1. Choosing Memory-Efficient Data Structures

The choice of data structure plays a significant role in memory optimization. For low-memory devices, the following data structures are commonly used:

Arrays: Simple arrays with fixed sizes are often the most memory-efficient way to store data. However, dynamic arrays (like **lists** in Python) may not be optimal for low-memory devices, as they require extra memory for resizing.

Linked Lists: While linked lists can provide flexibility, they are generally memory-hungry due to the overhead of storing pointers alongside data. For constrained systems, **doubly linked lists** may be avoided.

Bitmaps/Bit Vectors: A **bit vector** allows efficient storage of binary data (true/false, 0/1), using just one bit per element.

This can save memory in applications such as flags or Boolean arrays.

Fixed-Size Buffers: For predictable, static data, using **fixed-size buffers** (predefined sizes) can be more memory-efficient than dynamically allocated structures.

2. Reducing the Use of Recursion

In embedded systems with limited stack memory, recursion can quickly lead to stack overflow, particularly when the recursion depth is large. Iterative solutions should be preferred over recursive ones, as they use a constant amount of memory for execution.

Tail Recursion: In languages that optimize tail recursion (like **Scheme** or **Haskell**), recursion may still be a viable option. However, most embedded systems do not perform tail-call optimization, so recursion should be minimized.

3. Memory Pooling and Resource Sharing

Memory pooling involves pre-allocating a block of memory at the start of the program, rather than allocating and deallocating memory dynamically. This can prevent fragmentation and reduce memory allocation overhead. **Static memory allocation** can help control memory usage in embedded systems, avoiding the need for frequent dynamic allocations, which can be inefficient and prone to memory leaks.

4. Data Packing and Alignment

In embedded systems, data often needs to be packed into the smallest possible size to save memory. This includes:

Packing data: Combining multiple values into a single data type (e.g., packing two 16-bit values into one 32-bit word).

Memory alignment: Ensuring that data is aligned properly in memory, so that each data type uses the least possible space.

Memory Optimization Techniques for Embedded Systems

Memory optimization in embedded systems goes beyond just using memory-efficient algorithms. It also involves careful management of memory resources during the system's operation. Below are some techniques commonly used to optimize memory in embedded systems:

1. Memory-Saving Techniques

Compression: Data compression techniques can significantly reduce the memory required to store information. For example, using **Huffman coding** or **Run-Length Encoding (RLE)** can reduce the size of data that must be stored or transmitted.

In-place Computation: Performing calculations or manipulations of data **in-place** (without allocating extra memory) can reduce memory usage. For example, sorting an array in-place rather than creating a separate array can save memory.

Eliminate Redundant Data: Avoid storing duplicate data. For example, in an image-processing application, removing unnecessary pixel data or compressing redundant sections can save memory.

2. Cache Optimization

Embedded systems often use **caches** to store frequently accessed data in high-speed memory for quicker access. **Cache optimization** techniques, such as **cache blocking** and **blocking algorithms**, help ensure that data is retrieved from cache rather than main memory, improving performance and reducing the need for large data structures.

3. Code and Data Sharing

In many embedded systems, especially those with limited memory, it is essential to share code and data across different parts of the system. For example, libraries and shared resources can be used across different modules of the system, reducing redundancy and memory consumption.

Shared Libraries: Instead of duplicating code across different modules, use **shared libraries** that are loaded into memory once and used by all parts of the system.

Memory Mapping: Use **memory-mapped files** to share data between processes without duplicating the memory space.

4. Memory Fragmentation Prevention

Memory fragmentation occurs when free memory is scattered throughout the system, making it impossible to allocate large blocks of memory. **Fragmentation** is especially problematic in embedded systems with limited memory.

Compaction: Periodically defragmenting memory or using a **compact heap** can help avoid fragmentation.

Fixed-Size Memory Allocation: By allocating memory in fixed-size blocks, it becomes easier to manage memory and prevent fragmentation.

Example: Data Compression and Optimization Algorithms for Limited Memory

In embedded systems, **data compression** can be crucial when there is a need to store or transmit large amounts of data with limited memory. One of the most commonly used compression algorithms for embedded systems is **Huffman coding**.

1. Huffman Coding

Huffman coding is an optimal method for compressing data by assigning shorter codes to more frequent characters and longer codes to less frequent ones. The algorithm works by creating a **Huffman tree**, where each character is assigned a unique binary code based on its frequency.

> **Space Complexity**: O(n) for creating the tree and O(n) for storing the encoded data.

> **Time Complexity**: O(n log n) for building the tree.

Example of Huffman Coding for Text Compression:

python

```
import heapq
from collections import defaultdict

class HuffmanCoding:
```

275

```python
def __init__(self, text):
    self.text = text
    self.frequency = defaultdict(int)
    self.build_frequency()
    self.huffman_tree = self.build_tree()
    self.codes = {}
    self.build_codes(self.huffman_tree, '')

def build_frequency(self):
    for char in self.text:
        self.frequency[char] += 1

def build_tree(self):
    heap = [[weight, [char, '']] for char,
weight in self.frequency.items()]
    heapq.heapify(heap)
    while len(heap) > 1:
        lo = heapq.heappop(heap)
        hi = heapq.heappop(heap)
        for pair in lo[1:]:
            pair[1] = '0' + pair[1]
        for pair in hi[1:]:
            pair[1] = '1' + pair[1]
        heapq.heappush(heap, [lo[0] + hi[0]]
+ lo[1:] + hi[1:])
    return heap[0]

def build_codes(self, tree, code):
    if isinstance(tree[1], str):
```

```
        self.codes[tree[1]] = code
    else:
        self.build_codes(tree[1][0], code +
'0')
        self.build_codes(tree[1][1], code +
'1')

    def encode(self):
        return ''.join(self.codes[char] for char
in self.text)

# Example usage
text = "this is an example for huffman encoding"
huffman = HuffmanCoding(text)
encoded_text = huffman.encode()
print(f"Encoded text: {encoded_text}")
```

In this example, we construct a **Huffman tree** based on the frequency of characters in the input text, and then we generate the binary codes for each character. The output is a compressed string that uses fewer bits than the original.

2. Run-Length Encoding (RLE)

For simpler datasets with repeated values (such as image data or sensor readings), **Run-Length Encoding (RLE)** can be a simple and effective compression technique. RLE works by encoding consecutive repeated characters as a single character followed by a count.

Space Complexity: O(n) for the RLE data structure.

Time Complexity: O(n) for encoding and decoding.

Example of RLE:

python

```python
def rle_encode(data):
    encoding = ''
    prev_char = ''
    count = 1
    for char in data:
        if char == prev_char:
            count += 1
        else:
            if prev_char:
                encoding += str(count) + prev_char
            count = 1
            prev_char = char
    encoding += str(count) + prev_char
    return encoding

# Example usage
data = "AAAABBBCCDAA"
encoded_data = rle_encode(data)
print(f"Encoded data: {encoded_data}")
```

In this example, we compress the string `"AAAABBBCCDAA"` into a more memory-efficient form: `"4A3B2C1D2A"`.

Real-World Use Cases: Mobile Apps, IoT, and Embedded Systems

1. Mobile Apps

Mobile apps have limited memory and must be optimized for performance and efficiency. In mobile app development, **data compression** techniques like **Huffman coding** and **RLE** are used to reduce the size of assets (e.g., images, audio files) and improve performance. Additionally, **efficient memory management** techniques are employed to avoid excessive memory usage and ensure that the app runs smoothly even on low-end devices.

2. Internet of Things (IoT)

IoT devices typically have very limited memory, yet they must handle large volumes of data, communicate over networks, and perform complex tasks. Optimizing data storage and transmission is essential in these systems. **Data compression** and **efficient algorithms** for sensor data processing help reduce memory usage and bandwidth consumption.

> **Example**: An IoT sensor might use **delta encoding** to store the differences between consecutive readings, rather than storing all the raw data.

3. Embedded Systems

Embedded systems, such as **microwave ovens, washing machines,** and **smart thermostats,** often use small microcontrollers with limited RAM and processing power. Here, efficient algorithms for tasks such as **sensor data processing, control logic,** and **communication** are essential. Memory-efficient **algorithms** and **data structures** (such as **fixed-size buffers** and **circular queues**) help ensure that the system performs efficiently within its constraints.

Conclusion

In this chapter, we discussed how to design memory-optimized algorithms for **embedded systems,** focusing on techniques that help reduce memory consumption while maintaining performance. We explored how to choose memory-efficient data structures, optimize memory usage through preprocessing, and employ techniques like **data compression** and **in-place computation.** Examples like **Huffman coding** and **Run-Length Encoding (RLE)** illustrated how compression can be used in systems with limited memory.

Real-world use cases in **mobile apps, IoT devices,** and **embedded systems** highlighted the importance of memory optimization in ensuring that devices with limited resources can perform complex tasks efficiently.

By applying these memory optimization strategies, you can design systems that not only meet their functional requirements but also operate efficiently within the constraints of low-memory environments.

CHAPTER 26

REAL-WORLD CASE STUDIES OF ALGORITHM OPTIMIZATION

Algorithm optimization is a crucial element of system design and development across various industries. In this chapter, we will explore real-world case studies from sectors like **finance**, **healthcare**, and **e-commerce**, where algorithm optimization has led to significant performance improvements. These case studies will demonstrate how applying algorithmic techniques can enhance operational efficiency, reduce computational costs, and improve user experience. We'll also cover how these optimizations were implemented and their impact on the respective industries.

In this chapter, we will cover:

Case studies from industries like finance, healthcare, and e-commerce.

How real-world systems applied algorithm optimization techniques.

Examples: Optimizing search engines, recommendation systems, and fraud detection.

Case Studies from Industries like Finance, Healthcare, and E-Commerce

1. Finance: High-Frequency Trading and Portfolio Optimization

In **finance**, speed and accuracy are paramount, particularly in domains like **high-frequency trading (HFT)** and **portfolio optimization**. In these areas, algorithms must process vast amounts of data in milliseconds to make investment decisions or execute trades.

High-Frequency Trading Algorithms

In **high-frequency trading**, firms use complex algorithms to execute a large number of orders at incredibly high speeds. The challenge here is to optimize trading strategies for both **low-latency** and **high-throughput**, ensuring that trades are executed faster than competitors.

Algorithm Optimization in HFT: One common optimization technique is the **use of hardware accelerators** like **Field-Programmable Gate Arrays (FPGAs)** to minimize latency. These allow for direct data processing on hardware, reducing the delay compared to using software-based processing.

Impact: By using optimized algorithms and hardware, trading firms can process thousands of trades per second with extremely low latency, leading to higher profits and a competitive edge in the market.

Portfolio Optimization

Portfolio optimization involves selecting the best mix of assets to maximize returns while minimizing risk. **Markowitz's mean-variance optimization** is one well-known algorithm used for this purpose. However, as the number of assets grows, the algorithm becomes computationally expensive.

> **Optimization Techniques**: Techniques like **dynamic programming**, **genetic algorithms**, and **linear programming** are applied to optimize large portfolios efficiently. **Monte Carlo simulations** are also used to model the risk and return of a portfolio, helping to determine the best possible combination of assets.

> **Impact**: By applying these optimization techniques, financial institutions are able to handle portfolios with thousands of assets while maintaining acceptable computational costs, ultimately providing better investment strategies for their clients.

2. Healthcare: Medical Diagnosis and Treatment Optimization

In the **healthcare** industry, algorithm optimization plays a key role in improving diagnostic accuracy, personalizing treatments, and reducing healthcare costs. The goal is to process large datasets (e.g., patient records, genetic data, medical images) efficiently while ensuring the system's decisions are both accurate and timely.

Optimizing Medical Diagnosis Algorithms

Medical diagnosis algorithms, such as those used for **image processing** in radiology (e.g., **MRI scans** or **CT scans**), rely on deep learning models to analyze vast amounts of medical data. Optimizing these models is critical for real-time applications in hospitals and clinics.

> **Optimization Techniques**: In order to process images faster and more accurately, algorithms are optimized using techniques like **convolutional neural networks (CNNs)**, **transfer learning**, and **model pruning**. Additionally, hardware acceleration with **GPUs** and **TPUs** helps in speeding up computations.

> **Impact**: These optimizations have allowed healthcare providers to diagnose diseases faster, reduce human error, and provide better treatment plans, ultimately improving patient outcomes.

Personalized Treatment Optimization

Another area of optimization in healthcare is **personalized treatment** for patients. In this context, algorithms are used to tailor drug prescriptions and medical plans based on individual patient data, including genetics, lifestyle, and medical history.

> **Optimization Techniques**: **Machine learning algorithms** are used to predict patient responses to certain treatments by analyzing historical data. Techniques like **decision trees**, **random forests**, and **reinforcement learning** are used to make real-time decisions based on incoming patient data.

> **Impact**: By optimizing these algorithms, doctors can provide more personalized care, leading to better health outcomes and reducing the trial-and-error process of finding the right treatment.

3. E-Commerce: Recommendation Systems and Search Engines

In the **e-commerce** industry, algorithm optimization is crucial for providing customers with personalized experiences, whether through **recommendation systems**, **search engines**, or **dynamic pricing algorithms**.

Optimizing E-Commerce Search Engines

In e-commerce platforms like **Amazon** or **eBay**, search engines need to quickly return relevant products based on user queries. As product catalogs grow to millions of items, the algorithm's efficiency is key to providing a fast and relevant search experience.

> **Optimization Techniques**: Search engines are optimized using **inverted indexes** and **data partitioning** to speed up query processing. **Ranking algorithms** are optimized using **machine learning models** to rank products based on relevance to the query and user preferences.

> **Impact**: These optimizations ensure fast, accurate search results, improving the user experience and increasing conversion rates.

Recommendation Systems in E-Commerce

Recommendation systems are widely used in e-commerce to suggest products to customers based on their browsing history, preferences, and the behavior of similar users. Optimization of these systems is critical to providing personalized experiences that drive sales.

> **Optimization Techniques**: Collaborative filtering, **matrix factorization**, and **deep learning models** like

autoencoders are used to improve the accuracy of recommendations. Optimizations include caching frequently accessed recommendations, **dimensionality reduction** techniques (e.g., **Singular Value Decomposition**), and leveraging **parallel computing** for large datasets.

Impact: By optimizing recommendation algorithms, e-commerce platforms can increase customer engagement, reduce bounce rates, and ultimately drive more sales by suggesting relevant products at the right time.

Dynamic Pricing Algorithms

In competitive e-commerce markets, pricing strategies must be optimized to maximize profit while remaining competitive. Dynamic pricing algorithms adjust product prices in real-time based on demand, competition, and market conditions.

Optimization Techniques: These algorithms use **machine learning models** to predict demand elasticity, **A/B testing** for price sensitivity, and **price optimization algorithms** like **linear programming** or **genetic algorithms**.

Impact: The result is more efficient pricing, improved sales, and better market positioning for e-commerce businesses.

Example: Optimizing Search Engines, Recommendation Systems, and Fraud Detection

Optimizing Search Engines in E-Commerce

E-commerce platforms rely on fast and accurate search engines to deliver a seamless customer experience. Optimizing these systems involves reducing the time complexity of search queries and ensuring that the most relevant results are returned.

Inverted Indexing: For faster search query results, **inverted indexing** is used to map keywords to their occurrences in product listings.

Ranking Algorithms: These algorithms are optimized using **machine learning models** that rank search results based on relevance, taking into account factors such as customer reviews, product descriptions, and browsing behavior.

Optimizing Recommendation Systems in E-Commerce

Recommendation systems aim to suggest products to customers based on historical interactions. Optimizing these systems can lead to more personalized and effective recommendations.

Collaborative Filtering: This technique is optimized by using **sparse matrices** to represent user-item interactions and **dimensionality reduction** techniques like **matrix factorization** to improve prediction accuracy.

289

Hybrid Models: Combining collaborative filtering with **content-based** models (e.g., using product descriptions) helps further refine recommendations.

Optimizing Fraud Detection Algorithms

Fraud detection systems in finance and e-commerce rely on algorithms that can quickly and accurately identify suspicious activity, such as fraudulent transactions. These systems need to handle large amounts of transaction data while minimizing false positives.

Anomaly Detection: Machine learning models like **decision trees**, **support vector machines (SVM)**, and **neural networks** are used to detect unusual patterns in transaction data.

Real-time Processing: To optimize for **real-time detection**, fraud detection systems are often optimized with **streaming algorithms** like **Apache Kafka** or **Apache Flink**, which allow for processing large volumes of data with low latency.

Conclusion

In this chapter, we examined how **algorithm optimization** is applied in **finance**, **healthcare**, and **e-commerce** through case studies that highlight the importance of designing efficient algorithms in real-world systems. We explored how **search engines, recommendation systems**, and **fraud detection** benefit from optimization techniques such as **machine learning models, data partitioning, caching**, and **dynamic pricing algorithms**.

These case studies demonstrate how applying the right algorithmic optimizations can lead to better system performance, more accurate predictions, and an overall improved user experience. By understanding these real-world applications, we can gain insights into how optimization techniques can be applied across industries to address performance bottlenecks and improve outcomes.

CHAPTER 27

FINAL THOUGHTS AND FUTURE OF ALGORITHM OPTIMIZATION

Algorithm optimization has always been a cornerstone of improving the performance, scalability, and efficiency of computing systems. As we move into an era of rapidly advancing technology, the landscape of optimization continues to evolve, with **machine learning**, **artificial intelligence**, and **quantum computing** playing increasingly significant roles. This chapter will explore the **future trends** in algorithm optimization, the impact of emerging technologies, and provide key takeaways to help you continue improving your algorithms in the future.

In this chapter, we will cover:

Trends in algorithm optimization and future technologies.

Machine learning and artificial intelligence in optimization.

How quantum computing may impact algorithm performance in the future.

Key takeaways and final advice for optimizing algorithms.

Trends in Algorithm Optimization and Future Technologies

The field of algorithm optimization is constantly evolving, and as technology advances, new paradigms are shaping how we approach optimization. Several trends are emerging in the way algorithms are being developed, optimized, and applied across industries:

1. Parallel and Distributed Computing

As the **internet of things (IoT)** and **big data** continue to grow, the need for parallel and distributed computing systems is increasing. Algorithms that can run efficiently across multiple cores, processors, or even machines are becoming more common. This includes optimizations for:

Parallel algorithms: Designed to be executed simultaneously on multiple processors, these algorithms break down large tasks into smaller ones that can be solved concurrently.

Distributed algorithms: In large-scale systems, such as cloud computing platforms, algorithms are designed to run across multiple nodes in a network, improving scalability and fault tolerance.

2. Edge Computing and Optimization

With the rise of **edge computing**, which processes data closer to where it is generated (such as on **IoT devices** or **smartphones**), there is a growing need for algorithms optimized for low-power, low-latency environments. These algorithms must be lightweight and efficient to run on constrained devices with limited processing power and memory.

> **Optimization for Edge Devices**: Algorithms need to be designed for **real-time processing** while reducing the energy consumption of devices. Techniques like **low-power AI models**, **hardware accelerators**, and **model pruning** are becoming more critical.

3. Algorithm Optimization for Cloud and Serverless Architectures

In the cloud computing era, **serverless computing** and **microservices** architectures are gaining popularity. This trend requires the optimization of algorithms for dynamic scaling, cost-efficiency, and reduced latency across highly distributed systems.

> **Cost-effective resource allocation**: Optimization techniques are required to allocate computational resources efficiently, minimizing the time and cost associated with running algorithms on cloud platforms.

Serverless architecture: With serverless computing, tasks are dynamically allocated based on demand, requiring algorithms to be optimized for rapid deployment and minimal latency.

4. Data-Driven Optimization with Machine Learning

As data grows exponentially, **data-driven optimization** techniques are becoming more powerful. These methods rely on **data analysis** and **machine learning (ML)** to optimize algorithms based on patterns, trends, and performance metrics. Instead of relying solely on manually crafted rules, machine learning allows algorithms to adapt based on real-time data.

AutoML: With **automated machine learning (AutoML)**, tasks such as hyperparameter tuning and feature selection can be optimized without requiring in-depth knowledge of the algorithms themselves.

Machine Learning and Artificial Intelligence in Optimization

Machine learning (ML) and **artificial intelligence (AI)** are becoming central to algorithm optimization. AI has the potential to revolutionize how algorithms are designed, optimized, and deployed, enabling more effective solutions for a wide range of problems.

1. Reinforcement Learning for Algorithm Optimization

Reinforcement learning (RL), a subset of machine learning, has emerged as a powerful tool for optimizing algorithms in dynamic environments. In RL, an agent learns to optimize a process by interacting with its environment and receiving feedback in the form of rewards or penalties.

> **Optimization in Dynamic Systems**: In systems where decisions must be made in real-time based on changing conditions, RL can be used to adapt algorithms dynamically, improving their efficiency over time.

> **Example**: In a **cloud environment**, RL could optimize resource allocation by learning the best way to allocate computing power across a variety of tasks based on workload patterns.

2. Metaheuristics and Evolutionary Algorithms

Metaheuristics like **genetic algorithms** (GA), **simulated annealing**, and **particle swarm optimization** are used for solving complex optimization problems where traditional methods may fail. These algorithms often simulate natural processes like evolution and have been applied successfully in areas such as:

Combinatorial optimization: Solving problems like the traveling salesman problem (TSP), vehicle routing, or scheduling problems.

Machine Learning Model Optimization: Metaheuristics can be applied to optimize **neural networks, decision trees**, and other models, making them more efficient.

3. Neural Architecture Search (NAS)

Neural architecture search (NAS) is an emerging field where algorithms optimize the architecture of deep neural networks. Rather than relying on manual tuning, NAS uses **reinforcement learning** or **evolutionary algorithms** to automatically discover optimal neural network architectures for specific tasks, reducing the need for expert intervention.

Optimization in Deep Learning: NAS can automatically optimize deep learning models, making them more efficient and tailored to specific tasks, such as image recognition or natural language processing.

How Quantum Computing May Impact Algorithm Performance in the Future

Quantum computing is a revolutionary field that holds the potential to drastically change the landscape of algorithm optimization. Unlike classical computers, which use bits to represent data, quantum computers use **qubits**, which can represent multiple states simultaneously. This enables quantum computers to solve certain types of problems exponentially faster than classical computers.

1. Quantum Algorithms

Quantum computing is expected to lead to major improvements in algorithmic performance, particularly for problems that involve:

Factorization (e.g., **Shor's algorithm** can factor large numbers exponentially faster than the best classical algorithms).

Search problems (e.g., **Grover's algorithm** offers quadratic speedup for searching unsorted databases).

2. Optimization with Quantum Algorithms

Quantum optimization algorithms, like **Quantum Approximate Optimization Algorithm (QAOA)** and **Variational Quantum Eigensolver (VQE)**, show promise for solving NP-hard problems that are otherwise computationally expensive on classical computers. These algorithms can optimize complex problems in fields like:

Logistics: Optimizing supply chains, routing, and resource allocation.

298

Material Science: Finding the most efficient configurations of molecules for drug development or energy storage.

3. Challenges and Potential

Although quantum computing holds incredible promise, the technology is still in its infancy. Practical, large-scale quantum computers capable of solving real-world problems remain elusive. However, advancements in quantum algorithms will continue to shape future optimization efforts.

Key Takeaways and Final Advice for Optimizing Algorithms

As we look towards the future of algorithm optimization, several key takeaways can guide how we approach algorithm design and optimization:

Embrace Emerging Technologies: Keep an eye on the latest trends, including **AI-driven optimization**, **quantum computing**, and **parallel/distributed computing**. These technologies are likely to shape the future of optimization.

Focus on Scalability: As data grows and systems become more complex, scalability is essential. Always consider how your algorithms will perform with large datasets and high concurrency.

Data-Driven Decision Making: Use data to inform algorithmic decisions. Machine learning techniques like reinforcement learning and metaheuristics are becoming increasingly valuable for optimizing algorithms in real-time.

Efficient Resource Management: In the context of **IoT**, **mobile apps**, and **edge computing**, optimizing for memory, processing power, and energy consumption is just as important as optimizing for speed and accuracy.

Consider Quantum Computing: While quantum computing is still in early stages, learning about quantum algorithms and their potential impact on optimization will give you a competitive advantage as the field develops.

Conclusion

In this chapter, we explored the future of **algorithm optimization** and the role of emerging technologies like **machine learning**, **artificial intelligence**, and **quantum computing**. As we continue to push the boundaries of computation, the optimization techniques of tomorrow will be driven by intelligent, data-driven methods, quantum principles, and distributed systems that can scale across massive datasets.

For now, the key to mastering algorithm optimization lies in embracing **innovative techniques**, keeping an eye on technological advances, and understanding how new paradigms can enhance the performance and scalability of algorithms across industries.

By applying these strategies, you can stay ahead of the curve and design algorithms that are not only efficient but also future-proof, ready to take advantage of the exciting opportunities ahead.